Anja Langer

Language of Instruction and Cognitive Development

Beiträge zur Afrikanistik

herausgegeben von

H. Ekkehard Wolff und Hilke Meyer-Bahlburg

Band 21

LIT

Anja Langer

Language of Instruction and Cognitive Development

Case-studies from Malawi

LIT

Dedicated to my parents

Cover image: Rawlings Demba (†)

Bibliographic information published by the Deutsche Nationalbibliothek
The Deutsche Nationalbibliothek lists this publication in the Deutsche Nationalbibliografie; detailed bibliographic data are available in the Internet at http://dnb.d-nb.de.

ISBN 978-3-643-90344-0

A catalogue record for this book is available from the British Library

Klosbachstr. 107
CH-8032 Zürich
Tel. +41 (0) 44-251 75 05
Fax +41 (0) 44-251 75 06
E-Mail: zuerich@lit-verlag.ch
http://www.lit-verlag.ch

LIT VERLAG Dr. W. Hopf
Berlin 2013
Fresnostr. 2
D-48159 Münster
Tel. +49 (0) 2 51-62 03 20
Fax +49 (0) 2 51-23 19 72
E-Mail: lit@lit-verlag.de
http://www.lit-verlag.de

Distribution:
In Germany: LIT Verlag Fresnostr. 2, D-48159 Münster
Tel. +49 (0) 2 51-620 32 22, Fax +49 (0) 2 51-922 60 99, E-mail: vertrieb@lit-verlag.de
In Austria: Medienlogistik Pichler-ÖBZ, e-mail: mlo@medien-logistik.at
In Switzerland: B + M Buch- und Medienvertrieb, e-mail: order@buch-medien.ch
In the UK: Global Book Marketing, e-mail: mo@centralbooks.com
In North America: International Specialized Book Services, e-mail: orders@isbs.com
e-books are available at www.litwebshop.de

Contents

Foreword

Primary school education is one of the most essential pre-conditions for societal development. It is also the second of the Millennium Development Goals, according to which all children worldwide should have access to primary school education by the year 2015. Developments are measured through school enrolment statistics, the percentage of pupils who complete the fifth year of primary school and literacy levels amongst adolescents between 15 to 24 years of age (BMZ 2007). Malawi's recent education statistics show that a high percentage of pupils do not achieve their study goals and drop out of school within the first years of primary school. In comparison with the rest of the country, the percentage of school dropouts in the north and the area south of Lake Malawi is the highest. The presented study examines underlying reasons for this, yet the main focus rests on the language of instruction in early primary school years. To what extent does education in a familiar language influence the cognitive development of a child in the first primary school years? Are there differences in the development of cognitive abilities between children, who study in their mother tongue and children who are taught in a foreign language? How is logical thinking promoted in these different learning environments? What positions do different interest groups take on children learning in their native language and the consequential effects on their psychological development?

These questions are addressed in the following study. During the course of the research project, several academic libraries and collections were consulted. I was able to visit and research at the libraries of the *UNESCO Institute for Education* in Hamburg, the *University of Malawi* Chancellor College (Malawi), the *Malawi Institute of Education* in Domasi (Malawi), the *Polytechnic College* in Blantyre (Malawi) and the *University of Erfurt* as well as the *University of Leipzig* (both Germany).

The presented work was acknowledged as a dissertation and successfully defended on the 24th June 2008 at the Faculty for Art, History and Oriental Studies at the University of Leipzig, and published in German in 2010 (Langer 2010).

Acknowledgment

Professor Doctor Ekkehard H. Wolff I thank from the bottom of my heart for the supervision throughout my studies and the PhD.

The former GTZ Basic Education Programme in Malawi has provided the test in use called BIVA to analyze selected cognitive elemental operations. My sincere thanks go to the former GTZ-BEP Coordinator, Dr Wilfried Görtler and the Technical Advisor at Malawi Institute of Education, Dr Joachim Wagner.

I thank all the Malawian teachers and pupils for the unproblematic acceptance to actively participate in the tests and interviews as well as the community members, the parents and teachers of Chimbende, Kasolo, Ndengu, Mtuwa, Chombe, Mkombezi, Ng'onga, Chozoli, Chiole, Dombole, Bangala and Chilobwe for answering straight away my curious questions.

Furthermore, I thank my interviewees at Ministry of Education and selected Teacher Training Colleges for sharing their precious time and views with me; and Mr Rawlings Demba, a former illustrator at Malawi Institute of Education for fantastic materials. Special thanks to my research assistants Ms Bessie Chirwa, Mrs Catherine Mwanachawa and Mrs Linda Bwanali for very productive cooperation during the research trips.

During my 9 months research exchange at Chancellor College in Zomba, I was honoured to meet wonderful colleagues and friends, to name a few Mrs Stella Kachiwanda, Dr Dixie Maluwa-Banda, Prof Pascal Kishindo, Prof Alfred Mtenje and Mrs Nancy Mandiwa as well as a very special person to me, Dr Foster Kholowa who not only shared his office with me but read my scripts and constantly questioned my research findings.

Since our first meeting, Dr Hartford Mchazime and Mr Henri Chilora always answered my questions and were never tired of supportive advice. I will always be truly grateful. The colleagues at the Malawi Institute of Education, especially Dr William Susuwele-Banda, Mrs Kate Katete and Mr Davie Kaambankadzanja.

Malawi is a wonderful country and the friends that I met there – in the warm heart of Africa - Annie and Grace with their lovely families, my Malawian sister Catherine, Pastor Dan and Alick, to mention just a few, have made Malawi my second home.

My sister Karin Langer, my cousin Dr Frank Stummer and my friend Silvia Eckert never became tired of reading through my script, even with the added pressure of time and my impatience on their shoulders. Ms Sella Oneko did a fantastic job translating my German dissertation into English. Thanks to all of you!

Finally, my deepest thanks I owe to my family. My beloved grandma Annemarie, my parents Angelika and Reinhard Langer, my aunts, uncles and cousins for the continued and everlasting support.

1. Objective and methodology

This chapter explains the study objective and its academic significance in the field of African Studies. Moreover, the examined problem outline and course of the subsequent chapters are described.

1.1. Study objective

Despite efforts to integrate instruction in the mother tongue into Malawi's language policy, there are persistent opposing voices and objections from the country's political elite (Kishindo 1999:30). The present draft language policy in the education system states that, in the early primary school years, teachers should instruct children in the local language of the respective area, in order to promote the children's' psychological development by the best possible means (MRE 2007:2 ff). After attaining independence in 1964, Chichewa, the native language of Malawi's first president, Hastings Kamuzu Banda, was promoted in all public spheres. According to a resolution in the year 1968, other indigenous languages were officially banned from public life (Kishindo 1998:235). With the first free elections in the year 1994, Malawi's linguistic diversity was restored after the long ban. In the year 1996, thc government issued a directive, which prompted teachers to instruct children in a familiar language in the first primary school years (MoEST 1996). Very few official steps were however taken, to develop teaching materials and translate the idea of first language instruction into action in the aftermath of the resolution (Chilora et al. 2003:2). The language component was not incorporated into teacher training courses or the development of teaching materials, nor was it considered in the posting of teachers, so that some teachers were not conversant in their pupils' mother tongue. In the year 2000, for instance, 67 percent of all primary school teachers in Mangochi did not speak the local language Ciyawo[1] (Chilora & Harris 2001:4 f). This consequently means that a high number of primary school children are instructed in an – prior to school enrolment - unfamiliar language. Only about two thirds of the population speak Chichewa, the language of instruction, as their first language.

Studies in multilingual societies have shown that a child who is taught in a familiar language adapts faster to the school environment (ADEA 2006; UNESCO 2000a). As early as 1975, in his report "A Language for Life", Bullock demanded that lesson plans should reflect elements of the pupils' natural environment and that children should not be forced to discard their language and culture, when they begin school (Bullock 1975:543). In a multilingual society like Malawi this means, offering classes in the local languages. The

[1] Orthography according to: University of Malawi. Centre for language studies. The orthography of Ciyawo. E+V Publications. 2005. ISBN 9990891591.

more prominent Malawian languages have relatively distinct geographical boundaries and multilingual instruction is indeed feasible.

This study aims to examine the influence of instruction in the first language on the psychological development in three Malawian regions. It utilises a test, which examines children's problem-solving skills. Psychological tests have until recently only played a marginal role in African sociolinguistics. The study intends to analyse the development level of two groups of primary school pupils in regard to selected cognitive elementary operations. The utilised test, referred to as BIVA, is a picture-based intelligence test. In the subtests, it predominantly works with pictures. Beside quantitative evidence it also gives qualitative insights on cognitive development (Schaarschmidt et al. 2004:7). Children from the third and fourth years of primary school were tested in their logical thinking (independently from their school knowledge). Two groups of children were compared. The first group, henceforth referred to as the pilot group, received first language instruction in its early primary school years, while the second group, referred to as the control group, was not taught in the first language, but in the official language, Chichewa. Following a statement from the Ministry of Education in 1996 (MoEST 1996), language policy in Malawi has seen lively discussions (*The Nation* 21st June 1996; Kamwendo 2004:53 f; Kachiwanda, pers. 2006). The results of the study give further insight about a possible influence of the language of instruction in the first primary school years. They aim to substantiate decisions about education language policy, in discussion since 1996. The results also intend to give suggestions on how to ease the learning and familiarisation with the school routine for future pupils. The Malawian child stands in the centre of these observations. The study sets itself the goal to identify problems in the Malawian school system and analyse possibilities to improve early primary school education with a special focus on the language of instruction.

1.2. Problem outline

The education statistics for Malawi from 2006 show that 22 percent of the first year pupils interrupted their education (MoE&VT 2006a:37ff.) According to the statistics, family obligations including illness and domestic work, are the main reasons for school interruption during the first three years of school (MoE&VT 2006a:46). Furthermore, 26 percent of first year pupils in 2006 had to repeat the year. On a national comparison, the percentage of school dropouts and repeaters was the highest in the north and southern Lake Malawi-areas. The pupils in these two regions seem to have most difficulties in achieving their course goals in the first school years.

The Association for the Development of Education in Africa (ADEA), in collaboration with *UNESCO* and the *German Technical Cooperation (GTZ),* conducted studies in multilingual countries to examine strategies for optimal learning. According to the research, instruction in the first language of the pupils and teachers promotes the cognitive development of pupils and enables them to develop critical and problem-oriented thinking (Brock-Utne & Alidou 2006:91; Plüddemann 2005:203).

The presented study questions whether the use of Chichewa, a language previously foreign to the pupils, is a possible underlying reason for dropout and repetition of the school year. Earlier research projects on outcomes of first language instruction in Malawi have clearly shown that the pupils learn better when lessons are held in a familiar language, using appropriate learning materials (Kachaso 1988:18; Chilora 2007:39). The research on first language instruction in Malawi, described in Chapter Two, examines writing and mathematical abilities but logical and problem-oriented thinking do not represent a focus. In contrast, this study examined the possible influence of the language of instruction on schooling achievements and the development of selected elementary cognitive operations in early primary school years, in school children in Rumphi and Mangochi districts. It compares them to the results of selected schools in central Malawi. The difference between these schools lies in the local language of the school environment and the language of instruction in the pilot and control classes.

1.3. Research questions and hypotheses

The presented work aims to examine existing findings on the effects of instruction in the mother tongue in early primary school years in regard to the development of logical thinking and their relevance to the Malawian context. The main areas of interest are:

1. To what extent does instruction in a familiar language influence a child's cognitive development in its early primary school years?
2. To what extent are cognitive abilities developed in children who learn in a familiar language and to what degree is the same true for children who are taught in a foreign language?
3. How is logical thinking promoted in the different learning environments?
4. Which stance do various interest groups take on a child's education in the mother tongue and its effects on the psychological development?

The study aims to investigate whether pupils, who are taught in their mother tongue in early school years (referred to as the "pilot group") experience the same learning progress as pupils who are taught in an unfamiliar language from the beginning onwards (referred to as the "control group" in this study). Logical thinking or the ability to reason, and the test results are the same in these two pupil groups. With the help of statistical tests and on the basis of research results from various multilingual countries, this null-hypothesis will be verified or discarded.

In the following model, the accompanying alternative hypothesis is explained: it was assumed that pupils, who are taught in a familiar language in their early primary school years, achieve better results and display more structured logical thinking, than pupils who are taught in a predominantly unfamiliar language.

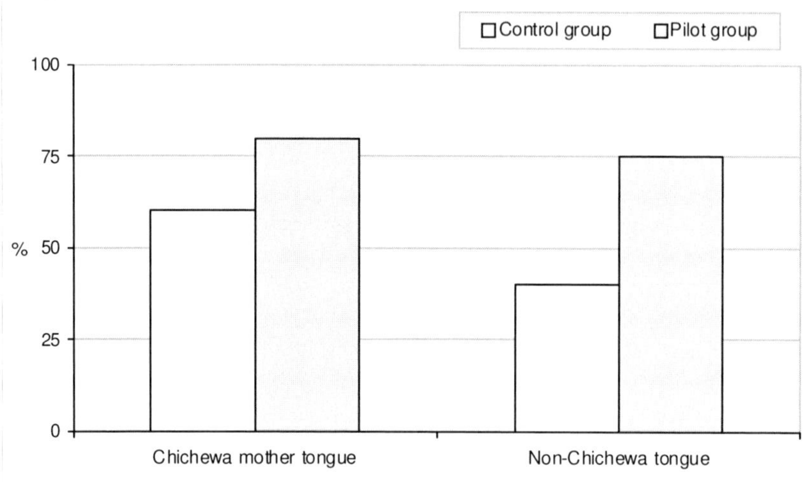

Figure 1.1. Alternative hypothesis model (Langer 2010:17)

The ordinate illustrates the results of the BIVA test in percentage and the abscissa shows the test groups. Chichewa mother tongue speakers and non-mother tongue speakers are tested. The latter named groups are Citumbuka[2] and Ciyawo mother tongue speakers. In order to control the hypothesis, pilot and control groups were formed and tested. It was assumed that:

1. The results amongst the Chichewa mother tongue speakers will not differ much.
2. The results amongst the non-Chichewa mother tongue speakers will show strong differences between the pilot and the control group.
3. The test results of the Chichewa mother tongue speakers are better than the non-Chichewa mother tongue speakers.
4. The results of the pilot group of the Chichewa mother tongue speakers are better than the results of the non-Chichewa mother tongue speakers.

[2] Orthography according to: University of Malawi. Centre for Language Studies. Citumbuka orthography. University of Malawi, 2005.

1.4. Methodology

The study is divided into four chapters and begins by presenting the research hypotheses and developing a model for better visualisation. The first chapter also explains definitions that become important as the study progresses. Chapter two presents a literature review of the topic, and theories of psychological development are set in relation to intelligence tests and research on multilingualism. Moreover, the language situation as well as Malawi's education system are presented and related to studies on the country's debate on language in the education system. The third chapter describes the empirical exploration, which attained its data through the use of a test and a questionnaire. An overview of the research area and the test population as well as the investigation's time frame is given. Valuable information was also gained during several personal interviews with linguists and pedagogues in Malawi. From the evaluation of the test data and the interview results, Chapter Four discusses conclusions for the practice as well as the limits of the research.

1.5. Terminology

Literacy describes a person's ability to read and write. Language is used as a psychological aid to extract meaning, experience joy and develop new thoughts from the read material. Simple messages are understood and can be passed on to others in writing (Krashen 1989:73).

The concepts of *bilingualism / multilingualism* describe an individual's or society's command or use of two or more languages. Individual multilingualism can be differentiated through the *time* of the language acquisition, the *degree of language command* and *language competency* (Baker & Prys Jones 1998:10,12,154; Hoffmann 1991:24). If more than one language exists in a certain area, one speaks of social multilingualism, which often goes hand in hand with diglossia. In such cases, languages are often used in functional distribution, meaning that each language has its own function and application possibility. The use of language usually depends on socio-cultural factors such as family, school, media, profession, cultural and religious activities.

When this study speaks of *mother tongue / first language / native language / language of play*[3], it describes the language the child uses in the home environment and when playing with friends. It is the language, which the child acquires first and it is usually the dominant or preferred language in a situation of balanced multilingualism.

Instruction in the mother tongue refers to lessons conducted in a language that is familiar to the pupil. In Anglo-Saxon literature, different words, for instance "home-language schooling" are used to describe this (Plüddemann 2005:203).

[3] Also: Language closest to the pupils

Through the use of a familiar language at school enrolment, conceptual development is not delayed. Through literacy in the first language, thinking structures are established and enable the transmission into other languages (Cenoz & Genesee 1998:28; Grundy 2000:97 ff.).

Cognition is a process, whereby information about one's surroundings can be gained, through learning, memorising, reasoning and problem solving (Goswami 2001:25).

In the mind, knowledge is represented in *categories* (Goswami 2001:53). Without the ability to categorise, everything that one experiences would have to be processed individually. By forming a general representation or a prototype of a class of objects or events, new impressions can be compared and integrated into a structure (Goswami 2001:53).

Cognitive development is the development of processes to understand a cause and effect relationship, for thinking, learning and judgement (Aitchinson 2003:31). Basic cognitive processes include learning, memory, perception and attentiveness (Goswami 2001:25). Higher cognitive processes, for example reasoning and problem-solving are built on this basis (Goswami 2001:53).

Cognitive psychology makes problem-solving processes, conceptualisation, awareness, memory, perception, decision-making and processing information a focus area of its research, in contrast to the concept of behaviourism, which examines the relationship between a stimulus, a reaction and consequences of an action.

According to Piaget's system, *logical thinking*, the ability to argue, prove, think and reason, develops in the phase of concrete operations (more on this in Chapter 2.1.1). Logical operations such as classification and the relationship between objects can be understood, yet it is bound to visible or easily imaginable objects. In the presented work and in the utilised tests, logical thinking is perceived as foresighted, deductive or inductive thinking. In other words it shows whether the ability to deduce from the general to the specific or the known to the unknown exists and can be transferred to a general situation. Logical thinking can be characterised through the generalisation of proven facts, the linking of different knowledge areas, foresight, reasoning as well as innovation (Bloom 1993:29).

In the classroom, logical thinking can be promoted by the teachers setting appropriate tasks. Explaining, reasoning, controlling and disproving are all actions which enhance logical thinking.

2. Literature review

The following chapter serves as an introduction into the subject matter and presents background information in order to gain a better understanding of the study. The chapter is sub-divided into five parts, which encompass psychological development with a focus on language development, intelligence and intelligence tests, multilingualism and multilingual schooling models, the language situation and the education system in Malawi as well as studies on multilingual education in Malawi.

2.1. Psychological development

The first part of this chapter, presents a small selection of the numerous development theories, focusing on approaches to language acquisition of mono- and multilingual children. What effects do these development theories have on lesson planning? How can the teacher support pupils in their psychological development? What influence does the language of instruction have on the development of selected elementary cognitive operations? These questions are discussed in the following sections.

2.1.1. Development process based on theories by Piaget and Vygotsky

The following section discusses some partially very controversial approaches to the development process. Three positions shall be presented.

The *behaviouristic* approach assumes the imitation of actions and examines the psychology of humans and animals by observing behaviour with the aid of scientific methodologies and the description of the visible. According to the behaviourists, every type of behaviour represents a building block in the stimulus–response chain (Cattell 2004:38). Advocates of behaviourism assume that human behaviour and the act of speaking are influenced by external factors. Burrhus F. Skinner [1904-1990] compared processes of conditioning in rats and doves to language development in human beings (Skinner 1957:462). Expressions and behaviour are stimulated through the sight of respective objects. According to this theory, a child acquires speaking through imitation. The child retains comments and phrases in the brain and recalls them in the appropriate moment (Cattell 2004:39f.) This would however mean that one would only be able to articulate those sentences that one has heard before and would not be capable of creating one's own sentences.

The advocates of *nativistic* theories chose an entirely different approach. They define development as the unfolding of genetic predisposition. On the subject of language acquisition, they claim that human beings have innate neurological abilities, which explains the ease and speed with which children acquire a language. Each person has a system, which enables him or her to develop the mother tongue through innate self-motivation, instead of learning or being taught the mother tongue (Chomsky 1972:100 ff.). Noam Chomsky developed the concept of *universal grammar* (Chomsky 1972: 120 ff.), which states that every healthy human mind develops a universal phonetic, universal semantic and universal syntax. With the aid of the universal semantic, the child acquires its language. It serves as a kind of template in the interaction between children and adults (Bruner 2002:102 f.). Chomsky described this type of template as a *language-acquisition-device-mechanism* (Chomsky 1986:4). The American Jérôme Seymour Bruner expanded the model and defined the interaction between adults and children and the related exchange of rules as a *language-acquisition-support-system* (Bruner 1986:77).

In contrast to this, representatives of the *cognitive* approach assume goal-oriented and self-regulatory actions of individuals. The interpretation of one's own experiences is the starting point of psychological development (Pflaum 1986:12). Active discovery of the environment and playing with other children are the preconditions for learning, while language acquisition is a subconscious process, which stands in contrast to the learning of a language, the process which leads to knowledge about the language (Krashen 1985:1). The work of two cognitive psychologists and representatives of this approach are described in the subsequent sections, as their ideas form the basis for this study. An active environment (Piaget 1992:176 ff.) and social interaction (Vygotsky 1978:27 f.; Bruner 1996:22) are therefore preconditions for the development of cognitive operations and higher levels of complex thinking.

The theory of the Swiss development psychologist, *Jean Piaget* [1896-1980] assumes a development continuum with unchangeable but varying aspects (Buggle 2001:24 ff.). According to Piaget, cognitive development is propelled through two adaptation processes, *accommodation* and *assimilation*, which take place when the balance between the organism and the individual is disturbed (Piaget 1992:10 ff.) Piaget understands accommodation as the adaptation of cognitive schemata to reality. Assimilation describes the interpretation of experiences with the aid of existing schemata. Most cognitive mechanisms already exist at the end of a child's first year and they are increasingly used (Goswami 2001:113).

Variable aspects of this development continuum are the structures and the cognitive contents, which are necessary for adaptation (Piaget 1967:102 ff.) According to Piaget, a child goes through four phases in the course of its psychological development. These phases are hierarchically structured and overlap each other. Each transition into a new phase involves reorganisations within the brain that determine what the child can learn in a certain context.

During the (1) *sensomotoric phase*, from birth until year two, the infant discovers its environment by touching objects and imitating persons who are close to them (Piaget 1951:6f; Bruner 1996:53 f.).The infant lives in the moment and cannot yet imagine that things continue to exist when they are not present. The newly born has simple reflexes and the ability to adapt to its surroundings.

Primitive reflexes such as grabbing, sucking and grasping become more complex and goal oriented.

In the (2) *preoperational period* from two to seven years of age, the child learns how to use conceptual actions, without being able to see or touch the object. During this phase, language and imagination are developed. Children discover their environment imaginatively through imitation and symbolic play[4]. When children imitate a person or a situation, they change their own behaviour. Through the imitation of activities, they expand their own behavioural potential. Actions and events from the real world are represented in the brain and are internalised. Internalisation is the basis for cognitive learning (Piaget 1991:64). While playing, objects and situations are assimilated and elements that do not fit into the activity are ignored (Piaget 1991:66 ff.). The children see events in relation to themselves ("egocentrism") and perceive their thoughts as unchangeable (Piaget 1992:193). In this phase, soliloquies or conversing with oneself acts as an agent between thoughts and actions (Piaget 1959:9 ff.) and are representative of active psychological processes, without stimulating psychological growth. Psychological growth instead is stimulated through play and dealing with objects during the soliloquies (Piaget 1991:64 ff). Children are mentally not yet able to maintain more than one relationship at a time. This leads to limits in thinking. They do not maintain one opinion, but take up different, possibly opposing opinions one after another (Piaget 1969:15 f.). Sentences with causal construction pose a problem to children in this phase because they may confuse cause and effect. They construct sentences such as "I lost my pencil, [because I am not writing]" (Piaget 1969:17). At the end of the preoperational period, children are in a position to give a reason for their claims and assumptions.

Gradually, they internalise patterns and schemata and at about the age of seven, they reach the (3) *phase of concrete operations*. At around seven years of age, children are able to organise knowledge in networks and to think in single steps. In contrast to the preoperational phase, a real action can be replaced through a mental action. Children utilise their logic for real or easily imaginable objects. They are able to comprehend and logically explain self-constructed sentences and analogies as well as differences between these.

In more recent studies, Goswami (2001:293) discovered that children could already deal with analogies from the age of two. The ability to combine, for instance enables them to imagine that the water content of two different glasses can be the same.

In the phase of concrete operations, thinking is increasingly guided by rules. The test persons of the presented study were in this phase. The utilised test examined, whether there are differences between the control and the pilot group (Chapter 3.1.) in pattern finding and translating these patterns into new problems.

---

[4] Characterization of games according to the respective development phase of the children: Piaget 1951.

From the age of twelve, abstract thinking develops in the phase (4) of *formal operations*. Children can now imagine different possibilities and do not depend on sizeable objects. They can put forward hypotheses and prove these systematically: They can also think about less obvious alternatives. They learn anticipatory planning and can solve problems on a theoretical basis.[5]

While for Piaget, the forces within the child have a significant influence on the development of a child, the Russian development psychologist, *Lev Vygotsky* [1896-1934], attributes a high importance to the forces outside the child (Vygotsky 1978:27). He described the development of elementary mental functions such as sucking and crying to more complex mental functions such as problem solving, creativity and imagination (Vygotsky 1978), which are only attainable through the use of language. In contrast to Piaget, Vygotsky sees soliloquies as the first indicators for internalised thinking (Vygotsky 1962:149). Children face problems and try to find solutions by themselves or through the consultation of adults. The meaning of words is deduced by understanding specific situations, in which the words are used (Cummins 1984:225). According to Vygotsky (Vygotsky 1978:19 ff; Pflaum 1986:11 ff.), human beings are equipped with two interacting symbolic systems, signs and helping aids. Signs are internal representations, while the aids are objects and the local language, which help in the organisation, categorisation and integration of experiences. Adults name objects and activities with which the children are confronted and as a result the children learn the designated terminology. They internalise these and construct categories and patterns, with which they henceforth store knowledge and experiences. Categories are constructed on the grounds of recurring recognisable properties. Here similarities between the objects play a role.[6] One reacts to events, people and objects, not due to their singularity, but due to their affiliation to a certain class and their relevant properties (Klix 1993:370).

2.1.2. Language acquisition in monolingual and multilingual children

Vygotsky describes three stages in the development of speech (Vygotsky 1962:50 f; Lefrançois 2006:226). After the phase of social speech, which mainly serves to control other peoples' behaviour and the expression of simple thoughts and feelings until the age of three, comes the egocentric speech which serves to control one's own actions between the ages of three and six. It forms the transition from social to inner speech. This inner speech enables children to plan activities and to observe and direct thoughts and behaviour (Vygotsky 2002:80 f.). Through social interaction, the human consciousness develops (Robbins 2001:86) and meaning is derived. When talking to children, adults use a modified vocabulary that is characterised through repetition and circumscription in

[5] The observation of the development levels of Piaget's own children served as a template for his categorization. He does not differentiate according to academic or cultural surroundings. As a result, individual differences may arise.

[6] Due to similarities in form and function bicycles are categorized as bicycles.

order to ease the child's understanding through context related usage (Cummins 1984:225). Here, non-linguistic information helps to comprehend language and semantic (Krashen 1989:71). Toddlers are constantly exposed to spoken language through their siblings, parents and playmates and through this they learn basic elements of phonetics, grammar, syntax and semantics. Language is not learnt through the study of grammatical rules or memorisation of vocabulary, but through comprehending the encoded message of the language and delving into its deeper structure (Krashen 1989:70). With the aid of a language, a person learns to express and share with others what he or she already knows. Advancing into the deep structures of language is a necessary precondition for the learning of further languages. Relevant information is selected from the language environment and organised in systems, which become more complex in the course of development (Peltzer-Karpf & Zangl 1998:8 ff.). This is eventually followed by the differentiation into specialised subsystems. The constant reorganisation of the system following the uptake of newer information results in various organisational levels and supports the self-organisation and pattern formation[7] in the mind. Multilingual children should reach a certain language level, before they start learning a new language (Peltzer-Karpf & Zangl 1998:10 f.). This realisation supports the idea of first language instruction, as the child can attain a certain stage in language acquisition before the new language is introduced. The selection and differentiation of data into different systems as well as the simultaneous reorganisation demonstrates high neural and cognitive complexity in multilingual children in contrast to monolingual children (Peltzer-Karpf & Zangl 1998:19). Word-meaning, phonetics and grammar are developed through the interaction with speakers of the second language. Through this exchange with speakers of different languages, structures in the brain are developed (Wong Fillmore 1991:52f.). Weinreich (1953:9 f.) theorised three possible storage systems in the brain (cf. Beatens Beardsmore 1982:21 ff.). Type A describes a system in which the words and pronunciation are sorted according to language, meaning that "book" is saved under [buk] in the brain, while "Buch"[8] is saved under [bu:x]. In Type B, words are combined, meaning that "book" is stored together with "Buch", in combination with [buk] and [bu:x]. In Type C, equivalents from various languages are saved under the meaning of the words in the mother tongue, meaning that both [buk] and [bu:x] are stored under the entry "book". The language systems are therefore either moulded into one as seen in Type B and C or exist adjacent to one another as seen in Type A (Beatens Beardsmore 1982:21 ff.). In clinical tests, Penfield and Roberts (1959:251 ff.) and Lenneberg (1972:214 f.) discovered that a child's mind is more mouldable than the mind of an adult. Until the age of ten, children have no problem

[7] Self-organisation and pattern formation in the mind: 1. Context dependant categorization, 2. separation from figure/base, 3. segmentation of the input into groups, 4. recognizing characteristic traits, 5. discovery of rules and categories, 6. organization of function related hierarchies.

[8] German for book

acquiring other languages as easily as their mother tongue (Schönpflug 1977:126). Animated interaction in a language-promoting environment adds to the development of language structures. Earlier experiences are structured in schemata in the brain, which serve the interpretation of new events and problems (Cummins 1984:232). According to Cummins' Threshold Theory, the level of language command influences the cognitive abilities of the speaker. Balanced multilingualism thus leads to a more complex intellectual capacity and a higher bilingual competency (Hakuta 1990:58). Dominance in one language leads neither to positive nor negative effects on the intellectual capacity of the speaker, which resembles the competency of a monolingual person. A poor command of both languages on the other hand leads to negative cognitive effects and the speaker acquires a low competency in both languages (Baker 1988:174 ff.). The level a speaker can attain in the second language depends on his or her command of the first language (Baker 1988:177).

2.1.3. Research on multilingualism

A comprehensive study on multilingualism is one from the linguist, Werner Leopold, who in detail recorded the language acquisition of his bilingual daughter, Hildegard, in the United States of America (Hakuta 1986:47 ff.). He did not limit himself to the observation of the language acquisition but made a point of observing phonetic, semantic and syntactical aspects as well as her acquisition of vocabulary. In the first two years of her life, Hildegard was not yet able to associate languages with specific persons. As she grew older this changed and she found it strange, if her English-speaking mother spoke to her in German or her father spoke to her in English. Although Hildegard often resorted to code-switching[9] in the first years of her life, she never confused English and German pronunciation (Hakuta 1986:5). At the age of two years and two months, she was capable of differentiating between the languages and was aware that her mother spoke English and her father German. She demanded object descriptions in both languages. Owing to the necessity of learning two terms for one object, Hildegard separated abstract concepts from the real object at a very early stage in her development. In monolingual children, this intuitive feeling for a language develops two to three years later (Baker & Prys Jones 1998:72; Baker 2006:155). As Hildegard grew up in an English-speaking environment, in which only her father and occasional longer stays in Germany represented the relationship to German, the active use of both languages declined after the age of ten and English became the dominant language. As a general valuation, Leopold attributed the benefit of being aware of the abstractness of language to early childhood bilingualism (Hakuta 1986:47).

[9] The use of two or more languages within a conversation: between paragraphs, between sentences, within a sentence or within a word (cf. Khamis 1994:15).

An American, Madorah Smith, conducted the first comprehensive psychological study on multilingualism in the 1940s. As a result of an observation of one thousand speakers of different minority languages in Hawaii, she came to the result that multilingualism leads to a delay in language acquisition (Hakuta 1986:59 ff.). She counted the errors, made by multilingual children, rating code switching as one of them, and compared them to those made by monolingual children. Her study is an example of the behaviourist research approach, as it focuses on observable language behaviour. In the 1970s the attitude toward research changed, as psycholinguists began conducting individual case studies over a longer period of time and the conception of multilingualism changed (Hoffmann 1991:120 ff.). Vygotsky for instance perceived multilingualism as an expression of higher intellectual ability (Vygotsky 1962:110).

More recent studies on the first and second language by cognitive psychologists, assume that languages are stored under different systems in the brain - the first language is stored through implicit strategies[10] and the second language through explicit strategies[11] (Fabbro 1999:89). This could explain why pupils who perform well in foreign language classes have more difficulties in following day-to-day conversations (Fabbro 1999:101). Profound knowledge in the first language forms an important precondition for the acquisition of other languages. In contrast to first language attainment, these acquisition processes are consciously directed, while the acquisition of the first language forms and heightens this consciousness (List 1995:36).

Different aspects of language development in monolingual and multilingual children were tested in recent years (semantically, phonetically, syntactically). Two studies are presented here as examples. Ianco-Worrall (1972) tested monolingual and multilingual children in South Africa. She came to the conclusion, that multilingual children from four to six years of age made semantic distinctions, while their ages mates distinguished according to phonetical aspects (Ianco-Worrall 1972:1397 ff.). The possibility of having a comprehensive arsenal of categories, concepts and language aids at ones disposal, enables a higher intellectual flexibility, creativity and intelligence (Bleyhl 2001:8; Baker 1995:83). With the help of language, opinions and thoughts can be named and explained (Klix 1993:370). A study in England and Cyprus (Loizou & Stuart 2003:3 ff.) examined, whether multilingual children have a different phonological perception than monolingual children. Tests of monolingual and bilingual children showed that multilingualism in general and the phonology of the first language have an influence on the phonological perception of the second language. According to the study, a phonologically complex first language eases

[10] Intuitive usage of information leads to subconscious effectuation. This type of learning develops slowly and can be increased through practice or usage (Fabbro 1999:97 f.).

[11] Consciously acquired knowledge can be recalled and verbalised (Fabbro 1999:97 f.).

the development of the phonological consciousness in a phonologically simpler second language (Loizou & Stuart 2003:13).

2.1.4. Significance of multilingualism in education

What significance do these insights have for lesson plan development and teacher training? How can lessons be constructed in a useful and interesting way for the pupils?

A child's way of thinking is naturally experimental and active. Experiments and practical actions lead to the formation of psychological operations (e.g. classification of animals) and logical thinking (Piaget 1999:24f.) through the interpretation of experiences (Pflaum 1986:12). With the aid of already acquired knowledge (for example a familiar language of instruction), new insights are gained. According to Vygotsky, teachers and parents should set the children exercises that are neither too easy, so that they can be solved immediately, nor too difficult, so that they cannot even be solved with external help (Lefrançois 2006:226). During the learning process, there is a phase, in which the learner can carry out an action together with the expert, but is not yet able to carry lone responsibility for it. Vygotsky (1998:202 f; 2002:326f.) described this phase as the *zone of proximal development*, which he defines as the area between independent action and working under expert guidance. He divides the development level into two phases, the actual and potential levels. The level of actual development describes the process of solving a problem without external help. The level of potential development is attainable through the support of another person, for instance the teacher (Tharp & Gallimore 1991:45). During the phase of proximal development, a teacher can motivate his or her pupils and can encourage the learning process (Pflaum 1986: 11). If the exercise is accompanied by language, it can be discussed and corrected, leading to a deeper understanding of the action (Vygotsky 1962:59). If the new concepts should further the psychological development of the child, the communication between pupil and teacher as well as amongst the pupils, should take place in a language which is familiar to everyone involved. The use of a foreign language during the introduction of new concepts may result in the child learning through mimicry, without adding to actual conceptual growth (Collison 1974:455). The learning process is thus closely related to the language. Learning does not occur through a transferral of the teachers' knowledge to the pupil, but depends on understanding and actively coming to grips with the teaching material.

The aim of academic education is to train self determined individuals (Piaget 1999:14), who question existing ideas (UNESCO 1998), acquire knowledge intelligently (Weskamp 2003:9) and reorganise it (Lefrançois 2006:204). This can best be achieved with approach of the "new, active" school. Piaget (1999:14) places a focus on group work and self-determination. He characterises group work as voluntary collaboration of the pupils, which requires the willingness to cooperate (Piaget 1999:15 f.). A positive side effect is the moderation of egocentrism, as the situation demands the harmonisation of individual interests with the concerted discipline of the pupils. The group acts as an incentive as well as a controlling organ and aids in the formation of one's personality. Piaget understands self-determination as the independent organisation of the school discipline. According to him, this promotes the development of a sense of solidarity and justice.

In terms of constructivist teaching, modern pedagogy has developed from its initial interpretation of test results to the stronger awareness for cognitive and affective processes (ADEA 2003:54). For the formation of categories and coding systems as components of all psychological activities, the discovery of relationships and properties and the reflection on thinking processes must occur (Bruner 1996:19). Working out of personal interest is also important for a discovery-oriented lesson plan (Piaget 1972:154). Through the pupil's participation in the lesson and the learning process, he or she steps out of the role of the passive listener and recipient into the role of the active learner (Wolff 2002a:7 f.; Weskamp 2003:10 f.) Advocates of constructivism argue that a child should discover its environment while learning and should through this take an active role in the construction of knowledge (Piaget 1999:14 f.; Wolff 2002a:86 f.; Lefrançois 2006:220). The interaction with people leads to reflection and idea development about objects, actions, people and oneself. It is the task of the teacher to support the pupil in the discovery of meaning and the construction of reality (Bruner 1996:20) as well as facilitating situational, realistic, day-to-day related learning (Terhart 1999:643).

In Malawi, as in many other African countries (Schubert & Prouty-Harris 2003:11; Alidou & Brock-Utne 2006:85), the presentation of concepts and concept structure through the teacher is the main focus of the lesson, instead of the active acquisition of these concepts through the pupil. As the transferral of the teacher's knowledge without the activation of previously existing knowledge does not add to the development of complex thinking and speaking processes (Cummins 1984:228), studies in Malawian secondary schools showed that very few pupils had acquired the formal operational intellectual level, appropriate to their age (Mbano 2001: 279). Cummins (1984:229f.) criticised the fact that the reformulation of class exercises into smaller and simpler components and the teaching in a logical sequence is not compliant with the research findings on the psychological development in children. In learner-centred classrooms, the learning goals are oriented on the process and on complex thinking abilities, rather than the material that is to be taught. Analysing, synthesising and evaluating play a more important role there than reciting and learning by heart. The active occupation with the learning material supports both the development of the problem solving abilities as well as the formation of language structures in the brain if the pupils involved in the process are motivated enough to complete the set challenges with a positive attitude (Cummins 1984:233). Before the Primary Curriculum and Assessment Reform in 2007, teaching in Malawi was very exam-oriented and the teachers were required to convey the material in a traditional manner (MoE 1991:i). Traditional teaching was characterised by the pupils' obedience towards an authoritative teacher, who instructs the pupils (Piaget 1999:14). Instead of motivating pupils to make their own discoveries, the demonstration of knowledge was seen as the priority. The result was a display of passiveness, absenteeism and school termination (Pota 2001:145 ff.). Cummins' studies (1984:228) in other countries also showed the teachers' ambitions to follow the set programme instead of attending pupils' questions. Lessons should not be overburdened and should convey topics that are relevant to the pupils in a plausible manner. The difficulty of the set tasks should stand in relation to the pupils' age and learning level (Lefrançois 2006:221). Children should (a) be allowed to ask questions in order to receive information and maintain the social contact; (b) be able to address topics which are of interest to them and the teacher should expand on these; (c) receive different motivations for discovery and discussion; and (d) be offered a meaningful and innovating room for discussion, in which the teacher is responsive to the pupils concerns, instead of correcting superficial mistakes (Cummins 1984:228). Effective teaching methods offer the pupils a plausible set of topics, which are of interest and relevance to them, in a relaxed teaching environment (Krashen 1989:71 f.). According to Piaget (1999:18) the "new school", is characterised by the active participation of the children and spontaneous self-initiated work as a result of personal interest. Personal interest arises when lesson contents are conveyed in a familiar language and take the children's environment and enthusiasm for discovery into account.

2.2. Intelligence/ logical thinking/ cultural comparison

Following a definition of intelligence, tests to determine intelligence quotients will be presented from early 1800 to date. How have the tests changed? What needs to be taken into account when standardised tests are used in different cultural settings? How do different cultures define intelligence? How were effects of multilingualism measured over the years and how were these test interpreted?

2.2.1. What is intelligence?

"Intelligence is what you use when you don't know what to do"
(Jean Piaget)

Intelligence is a quality of an individual, which helps the organism to adapt to the environment through the effective realisation of the necessary and the rationalisation of unnecessary intermediary steps, after the psychologically dealing with a problem and creating a balance between new impressions and internalised experiences (Piaget 1992:14). An intelligent person understands differences and similarities, generalises, but can also accept exceptions to the rule, can act responsibly and can learn from experiences (Schank & Birnbaum 1994:72 f.). Efficacy in problem identification and problem solving, quick adaptation to new situations, combining and generalising learnt material are therefore characteristics of intelligent behaviour. Beside academic intelligence (school knowledge), more recent psychological theories examine intelligence of age (culturally acquired knowledge and its related memory and knowledge strategies), practical, social and emotional intelligence (the understanding of and the effective conduct with other people in everyday life) (Sternberg et al. 2000). The latter is often reflected, in the definitions of village communities who were interviewed in this study. Practical intelligence is basically "common sense" and is characterised by life knowledge and cleverness, as well as planning and synthetic thinking (Guthke 1996:104).

Since the 19th century, various intelligence tests were used to prove the intelligence of a person. These are presented in the following paragraphs. Lamberti, 2006, offers a very detailed representation of the development of intelligence tests in the space of time with several examples.

2.2.2. Intelligence tests through the space of time

In the field of psychology, the first tests were conducted in Germany, France and England about 200 years ago. The world's first Institute of Psychology was formed in Leipzig in 1879 under the direction of Wilhelm Wundt [1832-1929]. The first decades were mainly devoted to basic research through observation. These were concerned with finding regularities of psychological processes in human beings (Guthke 1978:98 f.). However Wundt's assistant, an American named James McKeen Cattell [1860-1944], was less interested in the regularities than the differences between individuals. He developed so called *mental tests* for college entrance exams. These tests examined stimulus identification and the speed of reaction, revealing that the tests gave no indications about the subsequent academic achievements (Lienert 1961:8; Lamberti 2006:15). The pedagogue and psychologist Alfred Binet [1857-1911] and the medical doctor Théodore Simon [1873-1961] on the other hand wanted to test complex mental abilities in order to identify children with intelligence deficiencies amongst children with low academic performance. The Simon-Binet-Test (1905) tested various challenges without referring to taught school material. The test mainly involved language tasks, which were solvable with the help of intellectual abilities, such as recognising and describing differences, filling in gaps in written texts, understanding and repeating sentences as well as language independent tasks (finding irregularities in a picture). Binet and fellow psychologists were interested in the development of the intelligence tests, which could be solved independently of academic formation and education (Binet 1927:82 ff; Guthke 1978:99). In 1937, Lewis Madison Terman developed the Stanford-Binet test, a verbal intelligence test, in which proverbs are identified, contents of hearing exercises are repeated and sentence and number memory is tested

(Lienert 1961:9). The American psychologist David Wechsler developed a series of tests for different age groups (Guthke 1978:106). The first test-battery (Wechsler Bellevue Intelligence Scale), a collection of partly already implemented tests, came out in 1937. In 1949 Wechsler developed a test, which examines the intelligence of children (Wechsler Adult Intelligence Scale for Children – WISC); in 1955, a test for adults (Wechsler Adult Intelligence Scale – WAIS) and in 1967 the Wechsler Preschool and Primary Scale of Intelligence (WPPSI) to test the intelligence of preschool children. All tests involve a verbal section and an active section. Yet all these predominantly language-based tests exercises were, to a great extent, dependant on the verbal education in school and at home. The Englishman, John C. Raven, developed a language and prior knowledge independent matrix test in 1971, which required the correct placement of a puzzle piece (Guthke 1978:107). The problem with intelligence tests is that different tests find varying intelligence quotients in the same person. They generally limit themselves to one aspect of psychological ability, for instance verbal communication, non-verbal communication, and problem solving abilities, creativity or memory. Many of the tests are closely correlated to the understanding or knowledge of a language (Mussen 1963:46) and moreover using "academic intelligence" (knowledge and strict logical thinking). They lack the connection to performance in everyday life, for instance practical knowledge, social intelligence and the ability to solve day-to-day problems (Guthke 1978:114).

2.2.3. Tests to examine the effects of multilingualism up to date

Intelligence tests from the 19th and early 20th century, which are specially targeted at bilingual individuals, assume a negative effect of bilingualism on the psychological performance (Saer 1923:37). Characteristically for this era, neither the socioeconomic background nor the schooling situation of the tested persons was taken into account (Baker 1988:9 ff.). The test language was the common language of the monolingual and bilingual test persons and often, the weaker language for multilingual persons (Macnamara 1967:125). The results of the intelligence tests influenced political decisions in the sense that multilingualism was perceived as a problem and therefore undermined (Hoffmann 1991:122).

In the early 20th century, the anthropologists, Edward Sapir and Benjamin Lee Whorf, set up the hypothesis, that the structure of a language influences the perception of an individual in a society (Carroll 1956:57 ff.) and that language is closely related to the culture and the mentality of the speaker (Wolff 1981:31). Accordingly, the structure of the language influences the reality and self-perception of the speaker (Carroll 1956:27). This "language-centred principal of relativity"[12] was often debated and its limits were identified. In Southern America, Whorf studied the language of the Hopi who despite having very different languages, display cultural similarities to the Hopi-Tewan (Bruner & Goodnow 1956:304 IN: Philp & Kelly 1992:11). With the aid of a meta-language for the data interpretation, analysing the psychology of an ethnic group through a linguistic study is difficult, as the evaluation may lead to unwanted interpretations. As words have denotative and connotative meanings, only the precise analysis of a language allows conclusions about its structure and semantic (Schönpflug & Schönpflug 1995:423). Lambert (1975 In Fthenakis 1985:200) decidedly chose to oppose the Sapir-Whorf hypothesis, reasoning that culture and language do not influence the form or structure of thinking, yet they influence a person's content of thinking and possibilities of expression.

In the 1960s, Elizabeth Peal and Edward Lambert conducted tests with multilingual children, in order to gain an insight into the relationship between multilingualism and intelligence. They came to the result, that multilingual children with a balanced command of both languages achieve significantly higher marks than monolingual children, especially when the tasks involve mental flexibility and concept development. Moreover they argue that a brain, which has already occupied itself with two languages, will have better problem solving capabilities (Peal & Lambert 1962:20). Other studies made similar conclusions (Ianco-Worrall 1972:1398; Ben-Zeev 1977:1016). They confirmed that multilingual children become aware of the different languages and can differentiate tones, vocabulary and grammar of languages between the age of two and three. They reach a higher degree of metalinguistic language consciousness (Hoffmann 1991:125; Cummins & Swain 1986:31), which means they are aware of the arbitrary nature of language (Vygotsky 1962:110), the word-object relationship (Cummins & Swain 1986:31), the ambiguity of words (Lightbown & Spada 2006:9) and the forms and functions of the language (Bialystok 1991:115). Metalinguistic language consciousness is characterised by a high degree of analytical language knowledge (Bialystok 1991:130). Multilingual children recognise the language as a separate system amongst many. They display a quicker acceptance of replacing the name of an object with another term (Ianco-Worrall 1972:1399). As they learn several terms for the same object, children who are exposed to two languages in their direct surroundings, firstly learn that language is abstract and contains symbol-characters. Secondly, they can switch from one language to the next with more flexibility (code switching). In their knowledge pool, they generally have two words for the same object or activity at hand. Studies show that there is no identifiable negative influence on the psychological development in a situation of balanced multilingualism (Jarvis et al. 1995:305; Baker 2006:147), instead a positive influence can be observed.

[12] "Language centred principal of relativity": everyone perceives and exclusively interprets reality in relation to the predetermined patterns, which the grammar of the respective language offers.

Multilingualism enables the speaker to think about language, which in turn promotes the development of concepts and the identification of rules (Diaz 1983:23ff.). In other words it furthers creative and analytical thinking about a language (Hoffmann 1991:124; Cenoz & Genesee 1998:24f.) and offers an insight into different cultures (Hoffmann 1991:5). This seems to be important in the Malawian context, as the traditional authorities observe a loss of culture and traditional values amongst the younger generation. Besides the loss of the language, the authorities probably also contemplated their own dwindling influence. This societal change offers opportunities for further anthropological studies. Language is a symbol of culture; it represents cultural values and is a part of the culture it symbolises (Fishman 2005:7). Besides offering a Malawian child the possibility of more effective study, the opportunity of learning in one's own language, allows for a better identification with one's cultural heritage.

2.2.4. Intelligence in cultural comparison

In her book "Intelligenz und Dummheit" [Intelligence and foolishness] (2004), the cultural anthropologist Ina Rösing discusses these concepts in different cultures and calls for an "ecological" environment-dependent definition of intelligence (Rösing 2004:227 ff.). The use of conventional intelligence tests would give very little evidence about a person's ability, without considering the basic problems of their respective environment. In a subsistence economy, the abilities to create balance and harmony as well as the exchange and transferral of information are very important. Rösing describes studies with the Baganda and Batoro of Uganda. These ethnic groups regard a person who acts slowly and thoughtfully, listens and thinks matters through, asks and compares, as intelligent (Rösing 2004:255 ff.). In these cultures, intelligence consists of five components - advisability, conversational abilities, politeness, goal-directedness and problem solving abilities.

In the here-presented study, both teachers and parents of Malawian primary school children were asked about their definition of intelligence and logical thinking. Teachers defined it as the exchange of ideas, straightforward, problem-oriented thinking. Parents on the other hand laid a special emphasis on the social aspects. To them, problem-oriented, foreseeing thinking as well as self-dependence and survival strategies, responsible behaviour, studiousness and a good hand for business, good ethics and respect towards elders, obedience as well as friendliness, characterise logical thinking and intelligence.

Serpell's study involving the Chewa of Kondwelani village in Zambia in 1982 came to the same conclusion. Serpell conducted these studies due to his dissatisfaction with the rating system in Zambian schools. Children, who were raised in villages, achieved lower results than children from the towns and their results in turn, were lower than European and American results (Serpell 1993). His interview partners equally viewed quick thinking and social responsibility as a definition of intelligence. The village members describe a person as *wanzelu*, if he/she is clever (chenjela) and trustworthy, listens, understands and obeys, is punctual and cooperates with others (*tumikila*). Serpell asked the adults in the village to choose a child from a homogenous group (same age and gender), to solve an imaginary task[13].

Serpell (1993:36) also interviewed a group of adults in the USA on what intelligence meant to them and received a very different definition: intelligence is when a person accepts others in their individuality, accepts one's own mistakes, shows interest in the world, is punctual and shows a social awareness. The comparison of the concepts of intelligence shows that a test, which is developed by American academics and achieves reliable results in America, cannot achieve the same in a culturally different environment. The low performance of the children in the villages can thus be attributed to the fact that the test was created for a different cultural setting (Serpell 1993:26).

The researchers' experiences show that the literal transferral of a "western" test into an African context is not only a risk; it is also unreliable – in the sense of the reliability criteria for empirical studies. The decision to use BIVA in this study is based on how it sets its tasks, which are to a great extent solvable independently of day-to-day experiences. Some images, animals and stories, which are unfamiliar to Malawian children were changed and adapted.

As this study analyses the influence of instruction in the mother tongue in relation to the development of conclusive and logical thinking, this culturally unspecific test proved very useful for the empirical research. In African sociolinguistics, intelligence tests have previously been used very rarely. The study examines a different aspect of first language instruction than previous studies, which mainly tested reading and writing abilities (2.5. in this study).

2.3. Multilingualism and instruction in the mother tongue

Research on multilingualism is a wide and interesting field, which has for many years enjoyed a central focus in sociolinguistics. Academic research in different areas (linguistics, psychology, pedagogy, sociology), gained both positive (Fabbro 1999:106 f.) as well as negative insights (McLaughlin 1987:1 ff.). Scepticism about multilingualism came from various perceptions (Webb & Kembo-Sure 2000:128 f.). Some of the objections are that (1) multilingualism demands more work from the brain than necessary, (2) multilingualism leads to mental confusion, as the child does not know when to use which language, (3) multilingualism slows down the correct acquisition of a second language, (4) multilingualism results in a split personality and (5) leads to cultural and political divisions (Webb & Kembo-Sure 2000:128 f.).

[13] If a house catches fire and there are only these children present which child would you send to call others for help? Why would you choose this child? – Which child would you want to stay with you to help you? - - Suppose you are washing your clothes and you see that the place where you usually spread them out to dry is muddy; which of these girls would you send to search for another good place to spread your clothes?

The subsequent chapters discuss instruction in the mother tongue in multilingual education models and offer an insight into the language situation in Malawi.

2.3.1. Instruction in the mother tongue

In the course of cognitive development, the language predisposition plays an important role (Oevermann 1971:319 f.), as impressions and experiences are structured and categorised. Knowledge of the mother tongue enables the speaker to reflect about this language and its abstract use, independently of any concrete relationship (Lightbown & Spada 2006:8 f; Krashen 1989:73). Language becomes an intellectual tool for the speaker, with which he/she can acquire knowledge. Once the speaker has acquired a structural depth in a language, he or she can use this for any new language (List 1995:35; Krashen 1989:73).

Meaning becomes deductable for the reader when the text, the book or the information brochure is written in a familiar language (Kelly 1974:249; Mchazime 2003a: 19). It is easier for a pupil to learn something in a familiar language. For a child just starting school, the familiar language is that which is spoken within the family and when playing with friends. If the language is unfamiliar the child is forced to guess the meanings. This disables the learning of basic skills in reading, writing and mathematics (Mchazime 2003a: 19). Prah (1995:49) is convinced that the performance of pupils in African communities would improve and their abilities could be used more effectively for problem solving, if they were taught in a familiar language instead of an unfamiliar language. The pupils would understand the set exercises and could address the set questions directly instead of first looking for the translations, suggests Bisika (1984:51 f.).

The importance of African languages in the education system, for development and advancement has been an issue in international conferences since the 1950s (UNESCO 1951; 1990 [Jomtien]; Accra Declaration 1996; UNESCO 2000a [Dakar]), whereby a minimum of five years of school as well as additive multilingual instruction (Cenoz & Genesee 1998:28) are necessary to acquire basic skills in reading, writing and mathematics. A shorter span of training leaves the possibility of falling back into illiteracy very probable (ADEA 2003:35; Thomas & Collier 2001:6).

The reality in Malawian primary schools shows that both the teacher and the pupils use the local language of the school environment during lessons. Besides the 60 percent of Chichewa mother tongue instruction, a further 30 percent of lessons are taught in other local languages (GTZ representative for education in Malawi, Dr. Wilfried Görtler, pers. 2005). When questioning the primary school teachers, it becomes apparent that the lessons are difficult to prepare, as teaching material is only produced in Chichewa and the teachers are forced to translate the exercises and stories into the respective local language in order to make the tasks plausible for the pupils. A primary school teacher in Chombe, the Citumbuka speaking area, estimates that he spends about half of his lesson time translating, in order to make the set tasks understandable for the pupils. Denying the pupils option to use their mother tongue during lesson time, results in the pupils being ashamed of their language and culture. The dismissal of the mother tongue through another language can lead to damaging cognitive effects, as the first language is cast aside before the children are able to grasp the deeper structure of the second language and have built up communicative competencies (Lee 1996:515). Only a good knowledge basis of the mother tongue supports the learning of a new language (Cummins & Swain 1986:3). The pupil learns to read and write in a familiar language. In an ideal scenario, this is his or her mother tongue i.e. the language that he or she acquires as a first language. The conceptual development and mental structures are promoted through the instruction in a familiar language. In contrast, the use of a foreign language slows this process down.

2.3.2. Multilingual education models

Development and retention of a child's mother tongue are the basis for his or her psychological, linguistic and mental wellbeing and should therefore find its place in the primary school programmes (Cummins & Swain 1986:97). School education is a combination of different factors that influence and depend on each other. Dunkin and Biddle (1974 in Baker 1993:238) developed a model that put influences from multilingual systems into perspective. The following model is based on the above, but accentuates the aspects that are important for Malawi.

In the multilingual model, the teacher's language skills play an important role, because his or her ability to effectively use the pupils' mother tongue is decisive for the better understanding of the pupils. The community's perception of education determines the pupil's motivation to attend lessons regularly and actively. Through the use of learner-centred methods, the pupil is actively participating into the lesson programme. The learning material makes sense in the Malawian context and prepares the pupils for work life after school (MoE 2004:v). Moreover, the population's attitude towards the local languages influences their function and significance during lessons (Kembo 2000:290 f; Roy-Campell 2001:186). Based on their own academic experiences in which local languages had no official function, especially the country's educational elite did not actively preoccupy themselves with their mother tongues. They spoke and continue to speak to their children in English (Roy-Campell 2001:186).

Multilingual education systems can be divided into strong and weak systems, depending on their linguistic orientation and aims, in other words, the aimed competency in the first language (see Baker 1993:153 ff.). Weak systems do not result in the pupils' balanced competency in both languages and instead aim at monolingualism or limited bilingualism. These systems include models of *submersion, transition, segregation and separation.* Countries, in which the official language does not coincide with the pupils' mother tongue, generally follow transition models that use the majority language or a foreign language as the medium of instruction during lessons and aim at a social and cultural adaptation towards the majority culture.

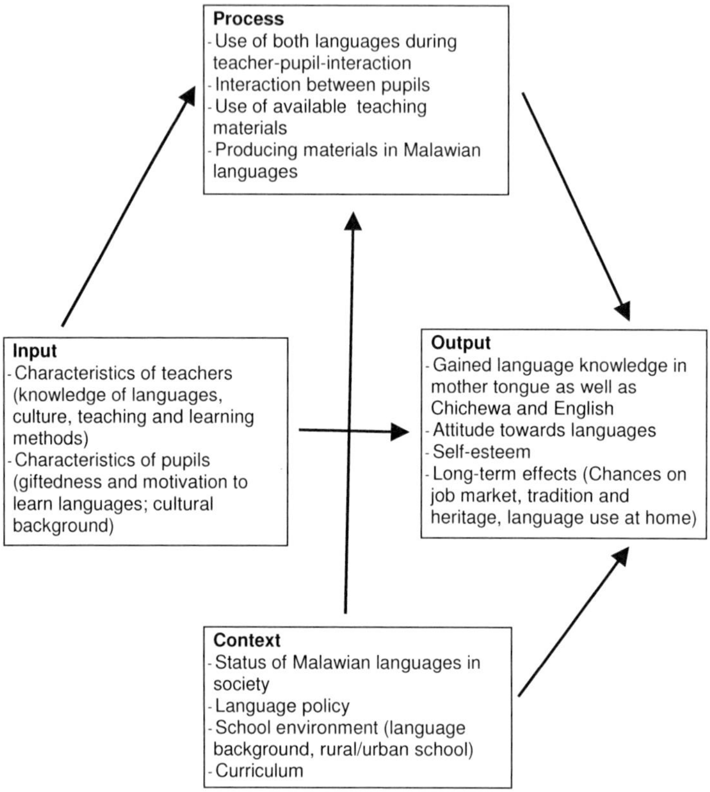

Figure 2.1. Influencing factors in multilingual school systems (Dunkin and Biddle 1974 IN Baker 1993:238)

In Malawi, Chichewa is the official medium of instruction in the first four grades of primary school. The submersion model, in which about 40 percent of the school beginners are instructed in a new language without having being taught the language beforehand, is used. Yet the reality is different. In the early school stages, teachers often utilise the pupils' mother tongue in order to ease interaction. The problems, which arise from this, are addressed later on in this study.

Strong multilingual school systems are characterised by aiming to achieve a balanced competency in the languages of instruction (Baker & Prys Jones 1998:469 ff.). This is firstly the children's mother tongue and secondly a foreign language (bilingual orientation), the official language (language preservation) or a majority language (immersion and preservation). The *concept of immersion* aims at an additive bilingualism and accentuates cultural diversity. *Language preservation programmes* use the pupils' mother tongue as the language of instruction in the first school years. The second language is initially introduced as a school subject and then takes up the medium of instruction role before the end of primary school. This concept promotes the acquisition of reading and writing competencies in the mother tongue and the subsequent transferral into the foreign language. Additive models aim at a balanced multilingualism of all members of society.

The Six Year Primary Project (SYPP) that was conducted in Nigeria in the 1970s showed that additive education models lead to a better learning performance (Bamgbose 1984:88 ff.).

Alidou and Brock-Utne (2006:75 ff.) examined the effects of the language of instruction in schools on the learning of the pupils, their behaviour and the classroom atmosphere and came to the conclusion, that a language of instruction, which is familiar to both pupils and teachers, has a positive effect. Through instruction in the mother tongue, new knowledge is combined with existing knowledge and independent, critical thinking is developed in the constant exchange with classmates. The pupils are talkative, eager to learn and enjoy sharing their knowledge. The classroom atmosphere is lively, cheerful and a trusting relationship is felt between the pupils and the teacher. Observations in classes with instruction in the first language were conducted before this study and supported Alidou and Brock-Utne's results. Classes, taught in the official language presented a different scenario (Alidou & Brock-Utne 2006:77). In these classes the pupils appeared apathetic, scared and showed a low self-esteem. They learnt how to obey, memorise develop survival tactics. The classroom atmosphere was tense, very calm and the teacher reacted defensively and not very supportively. Children however learn through active participation in the class (Cummins 1984:233).

2.3.3. Multilingualism in Malawi

16 languages are spoken in Malawi and Chichewa is the national language (Gordon 2005). As a former British colony, English also has the status of an official language. Linguistically and culturally, Malawi is closely related to eastern Zambia, northern Mozambique and southern Tanzania. Many Malawian Bantu languages are also spoken in these neighbouring countries. The Chewa, Tumbuka, Ngoni, Yao and Lomwe, who originated from the Congo basin, inhabited the region between the 13th and 19th century (Kayambazinthu 1998:370 ff.). The groups lived together peacefully and their languages had the same rights within the larger group. In the mid 19th century, Malawi was sought out by missionaries of various churches, who abolished slave trade and tried to evangelise the population (Kamwendo 2004:35 f.). They created schools in

which English was taught beside the local language. After a number of unsuccessful attempts to convert Malawians, they realised that to reach the people, they needed to learn and preach in their language (Kamwendo 2004:38 f.). The missionaries learnt the language that was spoken in their sphere of influence. They developed dictionaries and teaching material for the schools. The Scottish missionaries of Livingstonia mission, for instance, promoted Cinyanja, Citonga, Citumbuka and Cingoni, as their sphere of influence stretched from Cape Maclear along the lake up to the North. At the start of the 20th century, British colonial officers developed the idea of introducing a national language, which would be taught in schools all around the country and would function both as unifying and cost minimising (Kamwendo 2004:39). The government threatened institutions, who did not follow the official language policy with financial sanctions (Kamwendo 2004:40). The language community in northern Malawi protested against this colonial language policy and found allies amongst the Scottish missionaries. These feared the reduction of missionary conversions and school attendance. With the backing of the people, they achieved the recognition of Citumbuka beside Cinyanja.

After Malawi gained its independence in 1964, *Hastings Kamuzu Banda* (1906-1997) governed the country. In his efforts to unite the country, he declared his mother tongue, Chichewa, a dialect of Cinyanja, as the national language, while neglecting the remaining indigenous languages (Kayambazinthu 1998:370 ff.; Moto 1999:57 ff.)[14]. Dr. Banda established Chichewa in all areas, amongst others as the medium of instruction from Standard 1 to 4. In 1972 the *Chichewa Board*, a language committee, was assigned to work out rules of orthography as well as to compile vocabulary from the entire Chichewa speaking region with the aim of producing a "National Chichewa Dictionary". The national radio station aired educational and entertainment programmes in the national language, so as to establish the predominance of Chichewa speakers in the country's political spheres (Kishindo 1998:277). Other languages lost their official function and were only used in familial surroundings. The English language remained unaffected in Banda's language strategy and kept its unlimited functions. To this day it remains the administrative and governmental language and acts as the medium of instruction from the fifth grade onwards. Moreover, good English skills are decisive employability requirements. The association of power, success and prestige with the English language is deeply rooted in the minds of the people. Good knowledge of the English language opens the doors to social and economic success (Kishindo 1999:30; 2003:86). English acts as the main language in the most prestigious and important domains such as administration, education, justice, economics, media and government. Those who aim for a seat in parliament need to pass English exams and attain a minimum score in their final primary and secondary school exams.

[14] Critical analysis of the change from Chinyanja to Chichewa in Kamwendo 2001.

During Bakili Muluzi's period in office, from 1994 to 2004, the language policy was changed and linguistic diversity was promoted. Chichewa however, kept its status as the official and national language, as it was and is the most widespread language and is spoken by most Malawians as their first or second language. Yet the majority of the population would have still liked to hear their mother tongue spoken on the radio, in the health sector and in church (CLS 1999). In 1996, the government released a directive, which encouraged teachers to use the dominant local language as the medium of instruction in the first years of primary school (MoEST 1996). This was supposed to give the pupils the opportunity to participate actively in the lessons, instead of being hindered by the language they were still learning. Yet this decision, neither standardised teaching material nor lesson terminology in the different local languages are available (Chilora & Harris 2000:5). Malawian teachers indicated that for the better understanding of their pupils, they translate parts of the textbook during the lesson into the dominant local language, which takes up to 50 percent of their time (3.6.2.).

The above mentioned government directive often lead to public discussion about language policy in the media (*The Nation* 21st June 1996, 22nd June 1996; Kamwendo 2004:53f.; *The Nation* 6th December 2006, 23rd January 2007). Studies on instruction in the first language in Malawi clearly showed that a child could learn faster and better if he or she is taught in a familiar language in the first years of primary school. But among parents and teachers only English and Chichewa are believed to be the only valuable languages of instruction (*The Nation* 23rd January 2007). They have been taught like that. This opinion also prevails in other African countries and Kishindo (in press) explained its political motivation. In history, the choice of language created a type of wall against ones subjects, who did not protest and were employed as cheap labour (see ADEA 2003:41). The idea that the use of the local languages could divide a region is still widespread (Kamwendo 2004:39; Mtenje, in press). In interviews conducted for this study, this fear was voiced a number of times by primary school inspectors and district inspectors (3.6.2.). However, historical and present examples from around the world show that this assumption unveils an unfounded argument. Firstly, even monolingual countries have problems and wars (for instance Rwanda), and secondly there are many peaceful multilingual states, which promote multilingualism (for example South Africa). The fact that these fears exist in Malawi, underlines Wolff's demand for creating awareness and it backs his idea of social marketing as a precondition for an effective implementation of the language policy in the education sector (Wolff 2004:118 ff.).

Mtenje (in press) summarised the arguments for and against instruction in the mother tongue in Malawi during the Language Symposium 2006. Through a seamless transition from the home environment into the school environment, the children would be able to understand the teachers more easily, they would learn faster through more active participation and they would experience fewer failures or rejections, as they would understand the teacher's tasks and questions.

About 60 percent (Gordon 2005) of Malawian primary school children speak the official language Chichewa as their mother tongue and learn to read and write in this language. The other 40 percent acquire this language of instruction at the same time as the teacher uses it in class. Kamwendo (1997:207 f.) questioned the reasons, why the instruction in the mother tongue met such resistance and reasoned that the decision was made in March 1996, without the adequate sensitisation of the population, especially the teachers. The lack of teaching material in the local languages as well as qualified personal (Kamwendo 1997:208; Nyirenda 2003:124) made the planned implementation of the language policy in the existing education systems very difficult.

2.4. The Malawian Education System

The following chapter aims to present the Malawian education system. Education should prepare children for the future and should guide them on the right path to become involved in an active and efficient development of the country (MoE 2004:v ff.). The pupil must be able to use the learnt material in his or her daily life and he or she must realise the importance of lifelong learning.

The introduction of the multiparty system in 1994 also instigated some changes in the education sector. In the same year, the newly elected government declared free access to primary schools for all levels of society in Malawi. It abolished school fees and in doing so, enabled children from poor families to attend school. This bill was the direct answer to different international developments in relation to the "education for all" initiative, which was called into life in 1990 in Jomtien, Thailand, where 155 states pledged to (1) upgrade early infant education, enabling access for financially underprivileged families; (2) provide access to primary schools for all children and to enable the completion of primary school education; (3) improve the quality of education and to ensure that elementary skills in reading, writing and mathematics are attained with the completion of the education programme; (4) reduce illiteracy amongst adults; (5) improve the women's quota by means of enhancing gender equality; and (6) to create access to values and skills for a better, socially fairer life and sustainable development through various channels such as mass media, traditional and modern means of communication (UNESCO 1994:4 ff.). Two years after the opening of the primary schools for all children, the government decided to change the language policy in the primary school education (MoEST 1996). The decision was based on national and international studies on the influence of language in relation to learning performance and literacy (UNESCO 1962; UNESCO 2005:30). The SACMEQ studies (Milner et al. 2001; Chimombo et al. 2005a) showed that only a handful of primary school pupils attained basic skills in reading, writing and mathematics after the completion of Standard 5. In the year 2000, the literacy level stood at 81 percent for 15 to 24 year old boys, in comparison to 61 percent for girls of the same age group. This is an improvement in comparison to the 1990 level. The former level stood at 75.7 percent for boys and 51.2 percent for girls (Chimombo et al. 2005a).

2.4.1. Preschool

As mentioned in 2.4., the necessity of early infant education was already established at the World Education Conference in Jomtien in 1990. The early infant education lays the basis for learning later on in life and there are several efforts worldwide, to support children from underprivileged and poor families in their development (UNESCO 2007:9 ff.). In 1998, 5 percent of the children between the age of 3 and 5 were registered in preschools and nursery schools in the countries south of the Sahara - by 2004 this number rose up to 12.4 percent (UNESCO 2007:11).

The use of preschools in Malawi rose by 23.6 percent from 1994 to 1999 (United Nations 2001:24). According to the Association of Preschool Playgroups of Malawi (APPM), there were 113 preschool groups which were visited by 0.4 percent of the children from ages 3 to 5 during this period (UNESCO 2000b:chapter 8). These institutions are usually under the funding bodies of churches, village communities or non-governmental organisations and can predominantly be found in towns. According to a population count in 2004, 84 percent of the Malawian population live in rural areas (National Statistics Office 2004:10) and only have minimal access to preschool education. The demand for preschool education rose in Malawi with the opening of primary school education for all children in the year 1994. The rise in the number of pupils through the omission of school fees lead to a diminished teaching quality (Kadzamira & Rose 2003:504). As a result and due to the fact that preschool was seen as better preparation for primary school, the demand for preschool institutions increased (Kholowa & Rose 2007:462).

2.4.2. Primary school

Primary school generally takes eight years and is completed with the Primary School Leaving Certificate Examination (PSLCE). At the end of each year, pupils sit for exams that determine their transfer to next class. Pupils who do not meet the requirements repeat their year until they pass the exams. This results in the continuous rise in pupil numbers in the lower classes.

Figure 2.2. shows that 20 to 25 percent of the pupils in Standard 1 to 3 have to repeat these. Every fourth pupil for instance repeats Standard 1. This situation leads to enlargement of the class, as the pupils then have to sit in a class with next year's school beginners. This rate diminishes as one goes up the school ladder.

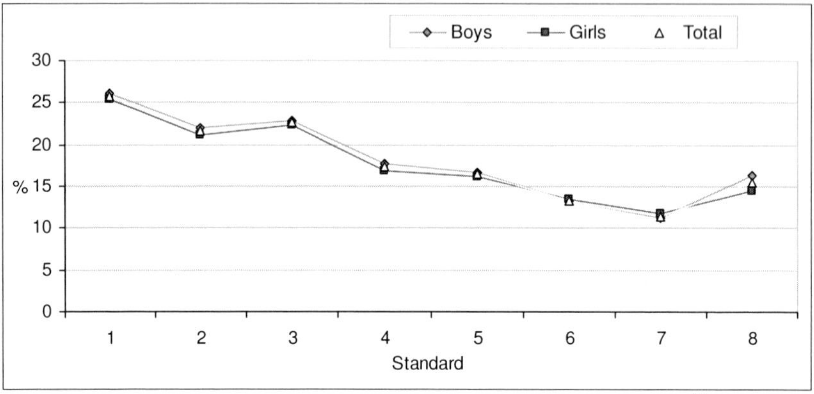

Figure 2.2. Repetition rate according to class and gender (Source: MoE&VT 2006:37)[15]

In Malawi, education experts [16]made the suggestion that the pupils who do not meet the requirements at the end of the school year should still be transferred into the next class in order to stabilise the number of pupils per class (MoE 2004).

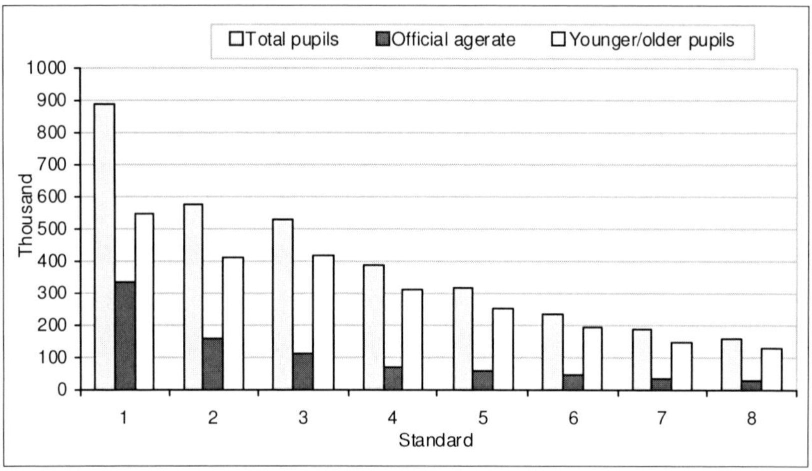

Figure 2.3. Age distribution in the classes (Source: MoE&VT 2006:41)

Figure 2.3. shows that in each class, the majority of the pupils are older or younger than the official age group of the respective class. Consequently there

[15] Tabular presentation in Appendix 10.
[16] Görtler, personal talk November 2006

can be age differences of up to ten years within a class. The different development levels complicate the choice of appropriate methods, to make lessons more interesting and effective. School beginners in Malawi are between four and thirteen years of age and they sit in one classroom. These children vary significantly in their intellectual performance level, as at the age of four, a child is just starting to comprehend the figurative meaning of words, while a thirteen year old generally has a much more complex mental ability.

At the age of five, children can use their first language correctly and can communicate effectively. They have implicit knowledge of the language, but cannot yet reflect on the language. At this age children begin to correct themselves. An eight-year-old child however has explicit knowledge of the language, knows the rules, can explain these and consciously thinks about language (see Three-Phase-Model on explicit Language Knowledge by Karmiloff-Smith 1992:48).

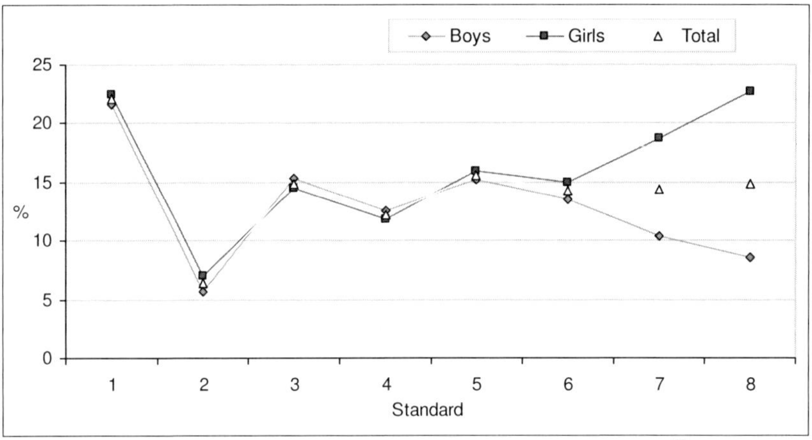

Figure 2.4. Dropouts according to Standard and gender (Source: MoE&VT 2006:39)[17]

According to the Annual Education Statistics 2006, the dropout rate was especially high in Standard 1 and Standard 8. Towards the end of primary school, it was predominantly girls who dropped out of school. Reasons for this are duties at home, early marriage or pregnancy as well as illness (MoE&VT 2006:46).

At the end of Standard 8, pupils sit for the final exam (Primary School Leaving Certificate Examination – PSLCE), which gives them access to a secondary school. In the year 2005, 67.2 percent of the pupils passed the final exam.

[17] Further details in Appendix 10.

2.4.3. Secondary school

The secondary school begins after Standard 8. It takes four years and is divided into two levels. The first level (Form 1 and 2) is completed with the Junior Certificate Examination (JCE). In the year 2005 57.2 percent of all pupils passed this exam. The second level (Form 3 and 4) is concluded with the Malawi School Certificate Examination (MSCE). In 2005, 38.8 percent of the pupils successfully passed their secondary school MSCE. Studies with Malawian secondary school pupils show that most achieved the concrete-operational level of thinking, but only a few reached the formal-operational level of thinking (Mbano 2001:279, cf. 2.1.1.). According to Mbano (2001:279 ff.) the teaching plan does not attain enough mental stimulation in order to reach this higher level of thinking, which promotes hypothetical problem solving and leads to abstract thinking.

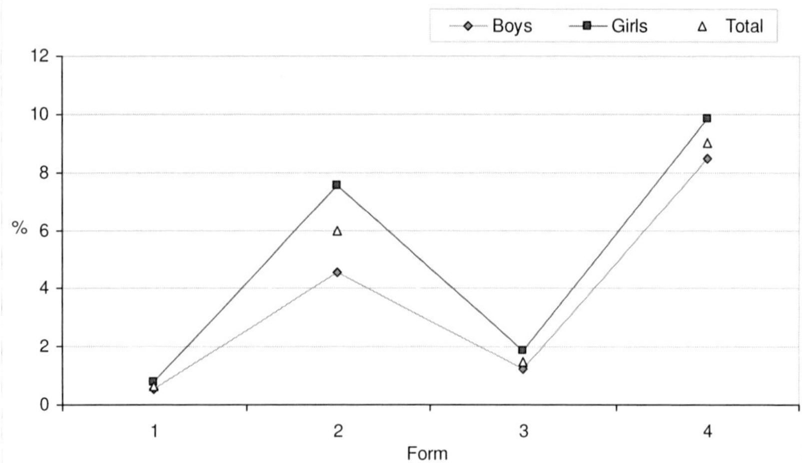

Figure 2.5. Repetition rates (Source: MoE&VT 2006:77)18

Figure 2.5. illustrates that the rate of repetition rose in the years in which the final examinations were taken. After Form 2, approximately 6 percent of the pupils were not transferred to the next level. In 2006 about 9 percent of the pupils repeated the final class of Form 4. Amongst these, girls showed the higher 9.86 percent in comparison to the boys who made up 8.47 percent.
Figure 2.6. shows that less than 20 percent of the pupils have the official age of their respective class level.

[18] Tabular presentation in Appendix 10.

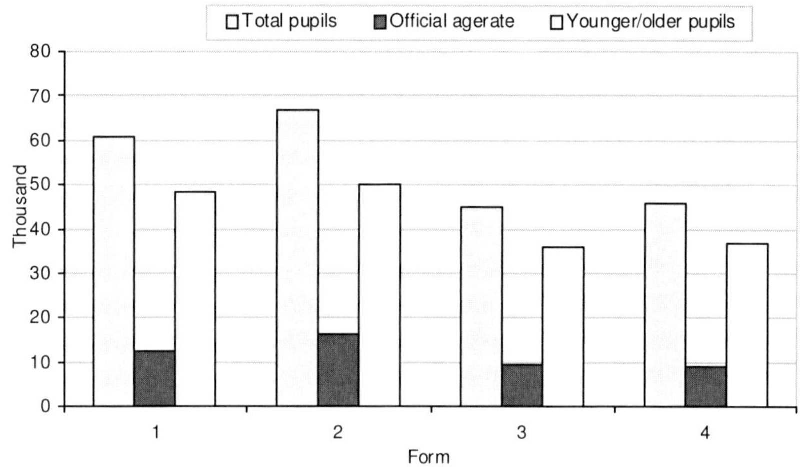

Figure 2.6. Age distribution in the classes (Source MoE&VT 2006:77)

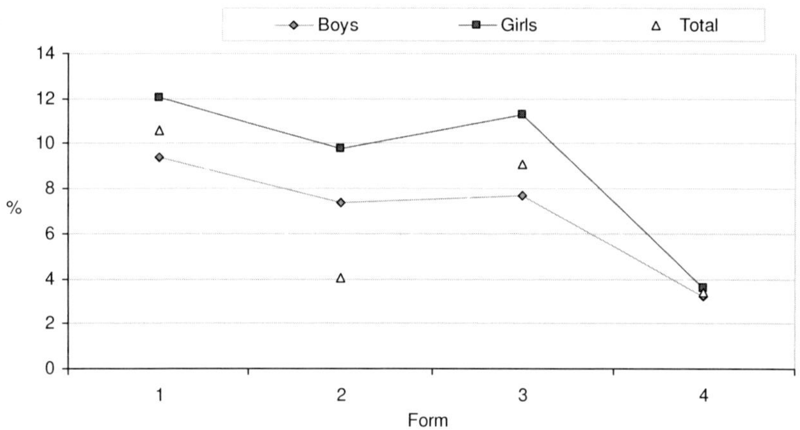

Figure 2.7.Dropout rates (Source: MoE&VT 2006:77)[19]

Figure 2.7. shows that more pupils tend to drop out of secondary school in the first three years, while the dropout rate in the final year is relatively low with 3 percent.

[19] Tabular presentation in Appendix 10.

2.4.4. Vocational training

When the requirement of trained personnel was recognised in the 1990s, vocational training centres which were co-financed by the state and the private sector were established. By then, approximately 22 professions trained their personnel during a four-year course. Amongst these were builders, gardeners, print-makers and carpenters. In this way, around 500 youths had the opportunity to learn a craft or technical profession yearly (UNESCO 2004:14). In the year 2000, the TEVET programme (Technical, Entrepreneurial and Vocational Education and Training –Programme) was called into being. The aim of the programme was to satisfy the market demand for qualified craftsmen and technicians. Besides the formal training, the programme also offers short courses to train youths in the informal sector. In the first five years, over 2500 youths were trained as tailors, bakers, soap makers, carpenters and builders (*The Nation* 29 April 2005). TEVET transfers youths to projects in their direct surroundings, in order to offer them a useful task with the possibility of real employment. Moreover vocational training places were created for youths with physical and mental disabilities.

Teacher training

With the introduction of free primary school education for all, the number of pupils rose from 1.9 million to 2.8 million within a year. Due to this quantitative expansion of the primary education sector, class numbers often rose to 120 pupils per class, especially in rural areas (MoE&VT 2006) and the lack of teaching staff became apparent (Kadzamira & Rose 2003:510). In the – by then - five governmental Teacher Training Colleges (TTCs), 3000 teachers completed their training after their two-year course (Kunje 2002:306). The government tried to meet the demand for teachers through training courses and it trained 18000 teachers on the job within a short period of time through the Malawi Integrated In-service Teacher Education Programme (MIITEP) from 1997 onwards (Kunje 2002:306). In 2002, 25 percent of the teachers described the training as effective (Chimombo et al. 2005a) and it has been replaced by a new training programme (Initial Primary Teacher Education – IPTE).). The IPTE-training is comprised of one year at a TTC and one practical year with regular supervisions through the college lecturers and support through a mentor at the teaching practice school. Each year, about 7500 new teachers are required to balance the demand due to illness and teaching staff affected by immunodeficiency, AIDS (Kunje 2002:317). Around 4500 new teachers are trained yearly through this programme and after only one year they are assigned to the country's primary schools for their second year of training. Since 2003, private TTCs exist beside the governmental ones. The currently six private TTCs train approximately 650 students per intake in two-year courses (Meyer, pers. 2013[20]).

[20] Personal conversation in April 2013 with Susanne Meyer, Technical Advisor in Teacher Education, GIZ Malawi

Additionally, the ODL (Open and Distance Learning) programme was introduced in 2010 to improve the pupil : qualified teacher ratio from 90:1 (in some districts 135:1) to 60:1 by 2013 and further to 40:1 by 2017 (MoEST 2010). The ODL teachers are oriented on pedagogical skills for 3 weeks before teaching, and during the following 30 months they are trained on the job with additional courses at the TTCs during school holidays. The first intake trained 3500 students on the job in 2010 and the following two years 11500 more teachers were trained in that way (DTED 2013).

2.4.5. Universities

In 2007 three universities existed in Malawi. The University of Malawi with its five branches[21] is the largest University beside the University of Mzuzu and the Catholic University Montfort. A regular study period at the universities varies from two to five years. In 2005, 5 percent of the Malawian youths with an MSCE secondary school leaving certificate, which is the precondition for a university acceptance, were enrolled in courses at one of the institutes (UNESCO Institute for Statistics 2005).

2.4.6. Additional education systems

As an answer to the requirements of school dropouts and adults in general, a number of non-formal education institutions sprung up beside the formal education institutes (Brock Utne & Alidou 2006:109). These institutions have an advantage over the formal sector, because they are more accessible, their teaching plan is adapted to the needs of the pupils and takes culture and surroundings into account (ADEA 2006:18). Yet like the formal education institutions, there is a small number of trained teachers, the teaching material is inadequate and teaching partly takes place in a foreign language (ADEA 2006:18). Non-formal education presents an overlap between formal and informal learning. Formal education is structured in a very hierarchical and chronological manner. It strictly follows the predetermined syllabi in schools and training institutes (Coombs and Ahmed 1974:8). Every organised learning activity outside this formal education system is termed as non-formal education. Non-formal education is conducted by community groups and organisations, follows preset learning goals and offers courses in the scope of adult education and qualification, also in public media (Elugbe 1996:28). Informal (indigenous) education is the ongoing learning process of each individual, interactions with family and friends, at work, in play and at the market. It does not follow a learning curriculum. Non-formal offers are more organised than informal offers, they involve specific goals, but at the same time they are more flexible than the formal education sector, with regards to age, duration, learning goals, methods and institutions (Hildebrand 1991:22). Non-formal education aims at social

[21] Bunda College of Agriculture, Chancellor College, College of Medicine, Kamuzu College of Nursing, Polytechnic.

change through strengthening the community and is therefore not always supported by the ruling elite (Hildebrand 1991:4).

One example of non-formal education in Malawi, the Complementary Basic Education programme (CBE), is described below. Young people between the age of 9 and 17, who have doped out and not visited a school for at least one year before the completion of Standard 5, visit a three year course, which covers the contents of the first five years of school. The CBE curriculum orients itself along the 2004 reformed primary school curriculum and places an emphasis on the command of the mother tongue and English, mathematics as well as four further chosen areas of teaching. Themes and problems of day-to-day life are treated as mainstream topics. In practice, CBE works very closely with local non-governmental organisations (NGOs) in the districts. Through CBE, pupils obtain the opportunity of returning to school and studying with their age mates. After the completion of the three-year CBE course, they have the chance to rejoin the formal schooling system.

2.4.7. Language in school

From Standard 1 to 4, the pupils are studying in Chichewa and all the teaching and learning material is available in this language. Chichewa is the mother tongue to about 62 percent of the Malawian population (Gordon 2005). In the first few years of school, the remaining 38 percent are partly taught in an entirely foreign language. English is introduced as a foreign language in Standard 1 and becomes the language of instruction from Standard 5 onwards. According to Baker's classification, this teaching model is a submersion model. Since the 1996 directive of the Ministry of Education, no measures were taken to implement the recommendation (Chilora et al. 2003:2). Teachers are stationed in understaffed schools, with no consideration of their language knowledge. The teaching and learning material is still produced in Chichewa. A study in the year 2000 showed that 67 percent of the primary schools teachers in Mangochi district did not speak the predominant language of the area (Ciyawo) (Chilora & Harris 2001:4 f). Instruction in the mother tongue is not addressed during the teacher training (Chilora et al. 2003:2).

2.4.8. Challenges

Schools fees have been eradicated in 1994 without the creation of the necessary conceptual and physical preconditions (KfW 2004:1 f.). Through the sudden rise in pupil numbers from 1.9 million to 2.8 million, the schools were neither equipped for the higher demand of classrooms and teaching material, nor did they have an adequate number of trained teachers. Schools consequently demanded a subsidisation of the water budget and sporting equipment from the parents, as well as the provision of building material and a workforce for building maintenance (Kadzamira & Rose 2003:506). Studies show that the ill-equipped schools with government teaching and writing materials, as well as the lack of money for school uniforms and learning material on the families' part, are major factors for absence and school dropouts (Kadzamira & Rose 2003:513).

Malawi is a country, which was hit very strongly by the HIV/AIDS epidemic. In Blantyre which is the most densely populated town in southern Malawi, three percent of all pregnant women were infected with the virus in 1986 – in 1996 this number rose to 30 percent. Teachers are among the high risk groups, whose death rate stood at a minimum of one teacher per district every fourteen days in 2002 (Kunje 2002:317). The age group of 15 – 49 year olds (encompasses more than 1.8 million people) is the group most affected by HIV/AIDS (Government of Malawi 2006:xvii) and the mother-to-child-transmission rate is extremely high. For many children, this means, that they have to contribute to the family income and care for ill relatives (UN 2001:4; Kadzamira & Rose 2003:507). Nearly every sixth Malawian household is headed by a child, who takes care of his or her younger siblings after the death of the parents (Government of Malawi 2006:xxii). In 2009, Malawi had about 650000 AIDS-orphans and the number is on the rise (Unicef 2009).

Besides the above mentioned issues, other factors also influence school life. In 1991 Nambuzi observed that Standard 1 pupils of Chikuli Primary School constantly came late to class. She discovered, that the pupils could not understand the mathematics teacher, who taught the first lesson and therefore they avoided the class. It surfaced that the teacher had previously taught Standard 8 and was not familiar with Standard 1 pupils (Nambuzi 1991). A study by Nantchito (1992) simply discovered that in the period of November to March, 200 of the 418 enrolled pupils were absent from the class, explaining that they had to help their parents on the fields. Had they gone to school, they would have had no food for the day. Moreover pupils had to take care of sick family members as well as attend funerals (Nantchito 1992). Other children feared the anger of their teachers if they came to school with dirty clothes or without writing material (Matunga 1992).

2.5. Malawian studies on multilingual education

Various documents criticise the low literacy level and call for a more effective school education (MoESC 2001; IMF 2002; Government of Malawi 2006). Reading, writing and mathematical skills are required in every aspect of daily as well as professional life. Chilora & Zembeni (2005:9) described the results of the SACMEQ study in 1995 and 2001 as extremely worrying, considering that most Malawian children drop out of school. In reaction to this discussion, the two following pilot projects were developed. With varying approaches, they have the same goal, which is to find ways to improve school performance in the early primary school years and to promote the psychological development of the children.

2.5.1. The "Literacy across the Curriculum" project (LAC)

The University of Malawi and the Malawi Institute of Education discovered that more than 70 percent of Malawians understand and use Chichewa, the national language. Children of a school age, however, have great problems and do not have an adequate command of the language required to follow the Chichewa-instructed lessons (Mchazime, pers. 2006). It was decided in October 2000 to examine the influence of the language of instruction on the learning performance in the early primary school years in a pilot study (Pfaffe 2000:268).

Study design

From 2004 to 2006, the project was conducted in 24 schools in three language areas - in the Northern Citumbuka speaking area, South of Lake Malawi, where Ciyawo is the predominant language and in Central Malawi in the Chichewa speaking area.

Six pilot and two control schools were identified in each area. The pilot and control schools varied in the language of instruction as well as the used methods of instruction. While the language of instruction in the control classes remained the national language Chichewa, the pilot classes were taught in the local area language. Following the introduction of free primary education in 1994, the extremely crowded Malawian school classes became accustomed to teacher-centred instruction. In the control group, this was continued, while the pupils in the pilot classes were encouraged to actively participate in the lesson programme. The teachers followed a teaching method, where the pupils learnt reading through writing. The classroom was divided into four different sectors and in each corner the pupil was expected to complete a different activity. The class was divided into four different groups and each group occupied one corner. After 20 minutes the groups would change corners accompanied by a song and a dance. There was for instance a reading corner in which motivational reading material could be found. There were activities for individuals as well as partners and groups. In another corner various writing activities, such as writing a story from a selection of pictures, were carried out. In another corner the children practiced mathematics with the aid of different materials for counting and problem solving. The teacher always worked with one group in the teacher's corner and covered new topics with the group or discussed problems that arose. Moreover, the teaching and learning materials were adapted to the language of instruction. For the schools in Rumphi, conventional books were translated into Citumbuka, the pilot schools around Mangochi were supplied with books in Ciyawo and in the pilot schools around Ntcheu, which lies in the Chichewa speaking region, the old school books were used. The teachers in the pilot classes were all mother tongue speakers of the region's predominant language and additionally participated in further training courses on teaching material development, so that creatively designed classrooms supported the learning process.

The aim of this project was to investigate whether children with Chichewa, Citumbuka or Ciyawo as their mother tongue showed a better learning performance if taught in their mother tongue as well as being taught through learner-

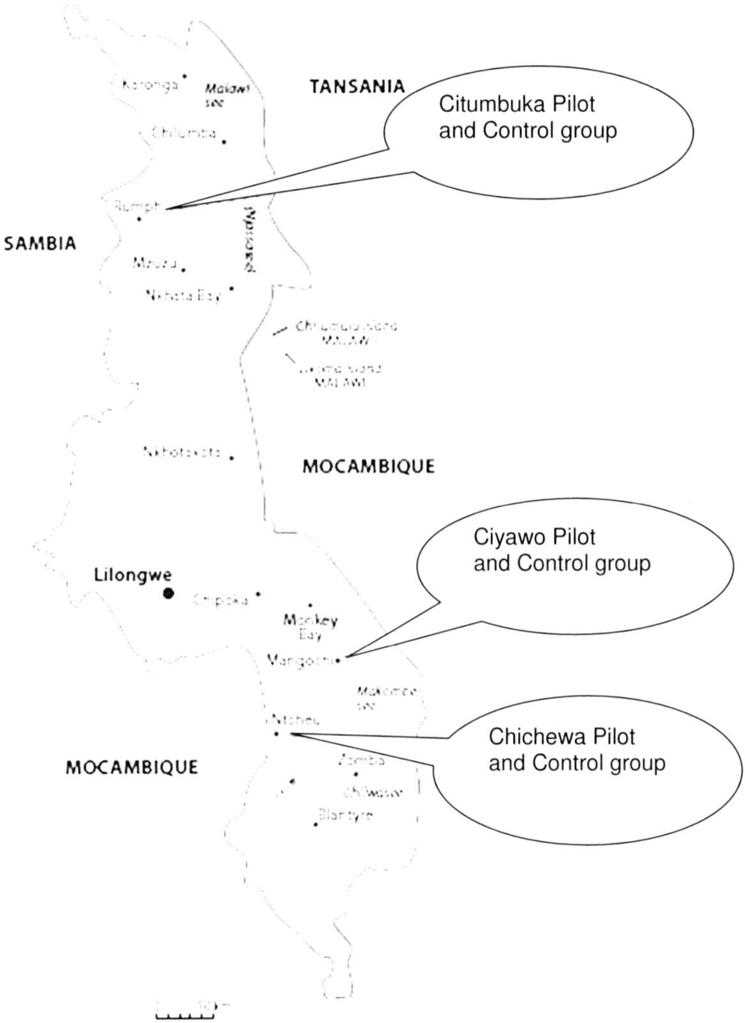

Figure 2.8. Map of Malawi (Langer 2010:58)

centred methods, rather than teacher-centred instruction. In the course of the study, the teachers were encouraged to enhance the pupils' participation in the teaching programme, to make the classes more meaningful and plausible for the children and to teach in the pupils' mother tongue (Mchazime, pers. 2006). In the first years of school the pilot pupils were only taught in their mother tongue and learnt reading and writing in this language. From Standard 3 onwards, they started with English lessons and in the case of the Citumbuka and Ciyawo speakers, with Chichewa lessons additionally.

Used materials

Both the pilot and the control classes followed the conventional curriculum, with the difference that the schoolbooks were translated into the predominant language of the area. The teachers of the pilot classes also developed additional material for the lessons and designed the classrooms in a pupil and learning friendly manner. In Standard 3, the pilot pupils could write their own stories, which were used to bring variation to the lesson plan (Chilora 2007:32).

Results

From school enrolment onwards the pupils of the pilot group learnt to read and write in their mother tongue. It was observed that the teaching of reading and writing skills was easier in the other languages (LAC-Coordinator Chilora, pers. 2006). At the end of Standard 3, the pilot pupils achieved better results in the English and Chichewa tests than the control pupils (Chilora 2007:32 ff.). It should be remembered, that the pilot groups in Rumphi and Mangochi only commenced English and Chichewa lessons in Standard 3, while the control pupils learnt these languages from Standard 1 onwards. The pilot pupils also showed a better performance than the control pupils in mathematical exercises and in their language of instruction, (Chilora 2007:37 f.). Moreover the repetition rate changed for the better. In the pilot classes, fewer pupils repeated the school year than in the control classes.

2.5.2. "Malawi Breakthrough to Literacy" (MBTL)

This teaching approach was developed in the course of the Molteno project in South Africa and has already been integrated into the curriculum of several southern African countries such as South Africa, Zambia, Namibia and Lesotho (Heugh 2006:62).

Study design

"Breakthrough to Literacy" is a course that integrates the children's former experiences into the syllabus. BTL is a method, which helps children to develop reading and writing abilities in their mother tongue in a short period of time. The approach places an emphasis on the hearing and speaking abilities that the children already bring from their home. The Malawi Breakthrough to Literacy was implemented as a pilot study in Malawi's Ntchisi and Zomba districts from August 2004 until July 2005. 153 schools participated as pilot schools. The participating teachers received training before each new topic from the Molteno-project staff, which could however not speak Chichewa. According to Chilora & Zembeni (2005:11), this at times made the training difficult and incomprehensible. 617 persons were trained before and during the project; amongst these were Standard 1 teachers, school directors, tutors, primary school inspectors, Ministry of Education staff and staff members of the Malawi Institute of Education.

Used materials

All teaching materials, with the exception of textbooks, were adopted from the Zambian Programme, Zambian Chinyanja New Breakthrough to Literacy (NBTL). The textbooks were translated from the South African originals and only reflect Malawian culture to a certain extent. The pupils were taught with a series of materials, such as posters, word cards, phonetic cards, exercise books, textbooks, slate boards and various other aids for sentence construction. All pilot classrooms were fitted with desks and chairs.

Results

The MBTL coordinator, Zembeni, left no doubt about the success of the project in both districts. According to him (pers. 2006), the majority of the pupils learnt to read and write full sentences and paragraphs and can even understand the read material. The approach apparently promoted the acquisition of reading, writing and mathematical skills in the local language. Critics of this approach say that the pilot pupils were indeed successful at the start, yet there were no sustainable effects in terms of additive multilingualism (Heugh 2006:74; Longden, pers. 2006).

2.5.3. Primary Curriculum and Assessment Reform (PCAR)

The pilot projects were timed so that their results could be considered in the primary school curriculum reform. According to the coordinator Kaambankadzanja (pers. 2006) the education reform was desperately needed, as the rise in the number of pupils since the introduction of free primary education in 1994 led to reduction in the quality of primary school education. In 2001, the Malawian government assigned the Malawi Institute of Education with organising the reform of the primary school curriculum with the aim of halting this negative development and adapting the contents of the 1991 curriculum to the current needs of the pupils and teachers. The new curriculum, which was introduced throughout the country in 2007, envisaged the entire development of a child within its environment and is less focused on examinations. The new knowledge has to be combined with existing concepts of education. The process of learning is weighted with as much importance as the knowledge at the end of the process (MoE 2004:xi).

2.6. Chapter Two summary

This chapter shows that the development of cognitive operations and more complex thinking processes benefits from an active environment and social interaction. An active exchange within a language-promoting environment supports the development of language structures.

The assumption that attaining a certain language level in the mother tongue is the precondition for learning a new language was demonstrated. The level of command of a language influences the cognitive abilities of the speaker. Hence a balanced multilingualism leads to more complex thinking abilities and a higher bilingual competency. A low command of both languages however leads to negative cognitive effects and the speaker reaches a low competency in both languages. Firm knowledge of the mother tongue presents an important precondition for the acquisition of further languages and for the expansion of the metalinguistic language awareness. This is characterised through a high level of analytical knowledge about a language. Studies have shown that balanced multilingualism has a positive and not a negative effect on mental development.

The development of a child requires a balance between assimilation and accommodation. In school, a child can incorporate new knowledge into his or her thinking with the aid of a familiar language. The use of a foreign language for the introduction of new concepts can lead to mere imitation, without adding to the actual conceptual growth. A child can learn with more ease in a familiar language. If the language is unfamiliar, the child may be forced to guess the meaning. This disables the learning of basic reading, writing and mathematical skills.

To what extent these findings are applicable for Malawi, will be discussed in the following chapter.

3. Empirical study

This chapter describes and discusses the process of data collection and evaluation, and presents an insight into the study area and the test population.

The study combines quantitative and qualitative methods to shed light on the influence of the language of instruction on the development of logical thinking and the test results. In the social sciences, the use of various research methods serves the investigation, explanation and planning of the complexity and richness of human behaviour from various perspectives (Cohen & Manion 1994:233). The aim is to find varying solutions for a question with the help of triangulation and to make the results comparable (Mayring 2002:147 f.). The presented study follows this approach. For statistical definitions used below, the works of Mertens 1998, Bortz 2005 and Schnell et al. 2005 give a comprehensive and easily understandable overview.

3.1. Data collection

In the presented study, quantitative material in the form of test results serves as the main source, while qualitative interviews serve the interpretation of the material.

The decision to not distribute questionnaires was based on two considerations. Firstly, the author had the opportunity to distribute questionnaires in ministerial and university circles during her Master-thesis and experienced a very low return rate. Secondly, the illiteracy level in rural areas lies at 41.3 percent (MoE&VT 2006b).

Observations of the lessons were conducted in both the pilot and control classes prior to the study and the gained insights served as a basis, but were not used as explicit research methods. As lesson observations bear the risk of distortion and are very time intensive[22], this means of data collection was not utilised.

The possible effects of the language of instruction on the cognitive development of children were studied in the following ways: One group of pupils was taught in their mother tongue, while another group was taught in a language which they were to a great extent unfamiliar with until school enrolment. After three school years, a sampling analysis in the form of an intelligence test was conducted in order to examine a possible influence of the language of instruction on the development of selected elementary cognitive operations. The test was developed at the Institute of Psychology of the University Potsdam and is not comparable to the conventional intelligence or aptitude tests in magazines. In

[22] Personal conversation with Dr. Foster Kholowa, University of Malawi, about his observations of preschool groups: The children only grew accustomed to the presence of the stranger after a number of visits. At first his presence had a relatively strong influence on the ongoing interactions.

this context, one should consider the discussion about the purely endogenistic interpretation of test results, which has accompanied the field of psychology since the beginning of this century. It reminds us that members of social or ethnic minorities as well as people who received little support are quickly categorised as less apt due to lower test results (Guthke 1996:143). The test used here is described in more detail below.

3.1.1. The test as a research instrument

Test or experiments serve the purpose of proving hypotheses (Schnell et al. 2005:65 f.) and were used in this study.

In 1984 Uwe Schaarschmidt and colleagues developed the BILKOG test at the Institute for Psychology of the University of Potsdam. This intelligence test was expanded and an image-based intelligence test for children of a preschool age was created (BIVA). Both BILKOG and BIVA are based on Klix's (1983) components of intelligence intensive processes, which are (1) the recognition of relevant characteristics or the suppression of irrelevant characteristics, (2) the recognition of the relationship between structures through comparison processes (Understanding of relationships) and (3) the transferral of relationships within one structure to another (analogy formation). BIVA focuses on the recognition of relationships between images. With the exception of the story section, the set tasks can be solved independently of daily life and the correct solution is deductable from the available material. The test analyses conclusive thinking, which is seen as the central function of mental performance (Schaarschmidt et al. 2004:11).

Quality criteria of the empirical research

At the start of this study, a decision was required as to whether a new test should be developed or a standardised, proven test should be used. The advantage of non-standardised tests is that they are specifically designed for a study and are suited to the test-persons. To fulfil the test quality criteria, *objectivity,* r*eliability* and *validity*, a series of pre-tests and specific considerations would have been required. At the end a prototype would have been established, which would have measured exactly what it had been designed for (Kranz 1997:4).[23]

As an appropriate standardised test already existed, the development of a new test was regarded as futile. BIVA provided the opportunity of a test, in which

[23] Objectivity is achieved if the results are gained independently of the evaluators and if different test-supervisors reach the same conclusion. The criterion includes the test phase, evaluation and the interpretation of the results. The reliability of a test describes the confidence in the results and ensures that the test-supervisor gets the same results at different points in time. Validity is ensured when a test actually measures what it is supposed to measure and blends out other aspects. Further literature on test-development: *(1)* American Educational Research Association, American Psychological Association & National Council on Measurement in Education. 1985. Standards for educational and psychological testing. Washington, DC: Author. *(2)* De Vellis, Robert F. 1991. Scale development: Theory and applications. Newbury Park, CA: Sage. *(3)* Gable, Robert K. 1986. Instrument development in the affective domain. Boston: Kluwer-Nijhoff. *(4)* Kranz, Helger T. 1997. Einführung in die klassische Testtheorie. Frankfurt / Main: Klotz.

solutions can be found through the available material independently of daily and school knowledge. Mental operations that form the basis of conclusive thinking as a central element of intelligence can be systematically differentiated. The test utilises pictures, some of which were adapted to the cultural situation in Malawi (*see* 3.1.1. *Adaptation*). From the original test, which is made up of eight subtests, four subtests were chosen for the study. The research assistants were encouraged to provide the same conditions for all participants in order to have comparable results. Through the selection of pupils from the LAC project, possible effects of independent variables were minimised, while the effects of dependent variables were maximised and unwanted disturbing factors were controlled. Independent variables i.e. conditions which were considered beforehand, are for instance the former academic education and the school's language of instruction. Dependent variables i.e. the effects that are to be examined in this study are for instance logical and problem-oriented thinking. Disturbing or unforeseen variables which can be controlled are the familial background and a possible balance between boys and girls. In this way alternative explanations can be eliminated. Kerlinger (1979) calls this the "Max-Con-Min-Rule" – maximising, controlling, minimising. Some information on the familiar environment of the pupils could already be taken from the project documentation, others were asked during the test. This for example included questions on the availability of books at home, the literacy skills of the parents, as well as the language spoken in the children's familial environment.

The Subtests

In the following section, the study's subtests are presented one by one by using images.

OHP[24] *--Isolating objects, positive*

The first subtest is supposed to familiarise the pupils with the unknown situation. In their daily life, Malawian primary school pupils rarely come into contact with industrially designed materials, such as puzzles, picture books and logic games. This first test, developed by the test-designers for younger children, proved to be a useful tool to overcome initial shyness and insecurities.

[24] German: Objekte Herauslösen, positiv

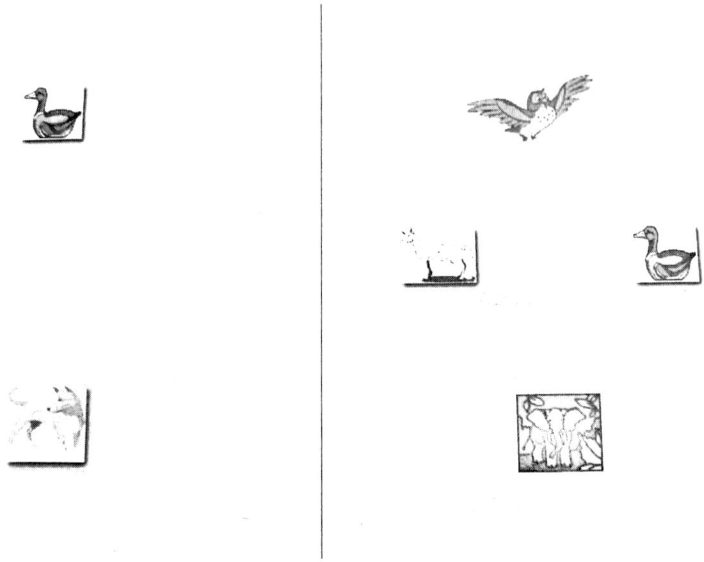

Isolating objects, positive[25]

An A4 card was optically divided into two halves, a green and a blue half. Each half showed animals, but only one animal could be found on both halves. The task was to identify or to point to the animal. The test person had to identify the relevant characteristics and name them. The dominant mental operation here was *isolation*.

GF[26] *–Pictoral stories*

During the second task, the child was given single cards, which told a story when organised in the correct sequence. The first card was placed in its designated position i.e. as number one. The child was then asked to arrange other cards on the table, so that they told a logical story. During this task, the child had to establish a correct cause-effect-relationship through the comparison of the cards. The aim was to recognise the relationship between the pictures and to place them in a logical order.

[25] Solution: The duck can be found on both halves.

[26] German: Geschichten Folgen

Pictoral stories[27]

RF[28]*- Continuing sequences*

For the third test, piles made up of four little cards each, displaying a cat, a chicken, a goat, a bird, a duck and a dog were placed in front of the child.

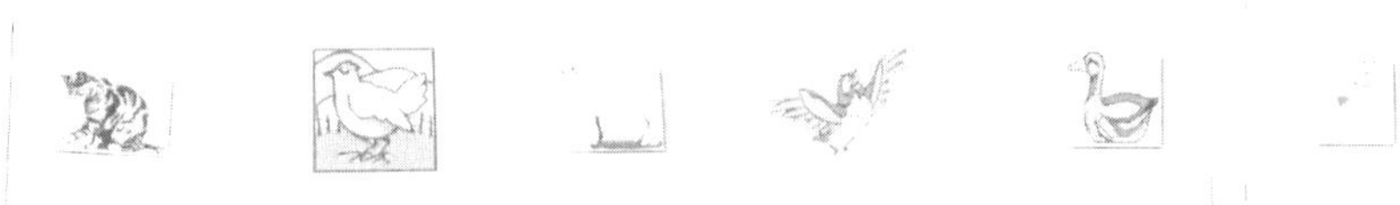

The test-supervisor placed three big cards in a row, one beneath the other, and explained to the pupil, that the animals were arranged in a certain order on those cards. It was the task of the pupil to continue the sequence by placing the correct little card(s) on the last big card.

The aim was to compare the order and to recognise the regularity or the changes of both the quantity and the position.

[27] Solution: Arranging the picture in a 1-3-4-2 sequence. (Alternative solution: 1-4-2-3).

[28] German: Reihen-Fortsetzen

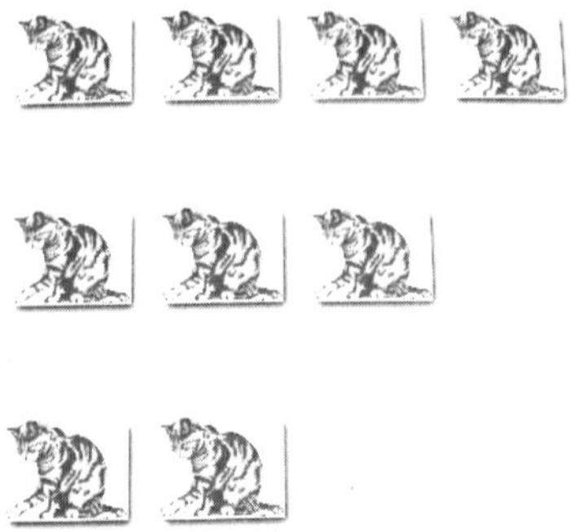

Continuing sequences[29]

RA[30]- Analogy sequences

For the fourth test, cards were again placed in front of the child, in this case four big and four small cats, mice, cows, beetles, fish, birds, goats, chickens, dogs and ducks.

Analogy sequences, example cards

The child was then given card A and A' on which the same animals were displayed in a different order and/or different sizes and/or different quantities. The researcher asked the pupil to describe the changes and tried to extract a rule of how and in which way card A changed to A'. In the next step, card B was uncovered for the child. B also displayed animals and the child was encouraged to describe the images.

The animals in B were supposed to be changed in the same way in which card A was changed to A'.

[29] Solution: A cat on the fourth card.

[30] German: Reihen- Analogien

The test person first had to compare the two cards (A and A') and articulate a rule. In this task, position, quantity as well as size relationships had to be considered, because besides the position and the quantity, the animals could also change their size. In an ideal scenario, the rule was consequently *transferred* and card B was transformed into B'.

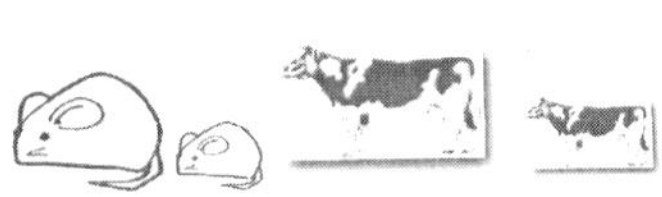

Card A

Card B

Card A'

Card B'[31]

Duration, assistance and marking

The selected BIVA subtests took between 50 to 75 minutes for each pupil, depending on the pupil's understanding and working speed. They were conducted as individual tests. BIVA offered the test-supervisor the opportunity to assist the child. Step by step assistance was given and started by simply pointing out a mistake, combined with the repetition of the main aim of the exercise and the encouragement to try the exercise again. If the test person came to the wrong conclusion again, the principle of solving the problem was clarified in cooperation with the test person, but the problem was to be resolved by the test person. If the tested child could not find a solution after the second aid, the problem was resolved for the child with a plausible explanation.

The test person could attain 0 to 3 points per exercise, with 6 exercises per subtest, resulting in a possible total of 18 points. Depending on the received assistance, the exercises were marked as described: 3 points were given for a correct result without help, 2 points were given for a correct result after pointing out the mistake and 1 point was given for a correct result after clarifying the problem solving principle. If the solution had to be explained, the test-supervisor gave no points for the respective exercise.

Adaptation

As the BIVA test was developed for German children, who grew up in a different environment than their Malawian age mates, some pictures and stories were changed into an African version. The test has been modified in collaboration

[31] Solution (from left to right): small beetle - big beetle – big fish – small fish.

with colleagues from the University of Malawi, Chancellor College and illustrators at the Malawi Institute of Education in Domasi.

The use of a standardised test requires the researcher's specific knowledge of the culture and empathy towards the other culture (American Psychological Association 1993; Ponterotto et al. 1995; Mertens 1998). There are psychologists who think it is absolutely absurd to study intelligence outside one's own culture or between different cultures. In 1974, Berry spoke of a radical cultural relativism and described this as the negation of any psychological similarities between different cultures. Intelligence should only be studied within one cultural setting and the transferral of standardised tests from one culture to another is not possible (Sternberg et al. 2000:28). This critique is probably by no means unfounded and was purposely considered during the selection of the test used in this study. Through the use of images, while avoiding the use of language, the BIVA test seemed transferrable to the Malawian setting. The pictures were adapted to the Malawian cultural context and the experiences of the pupils. In the described test, the following changes were made:

In the first, third and fourth subtest (OHP, RF, RA) pigs were replaced with cows, as pigs are rare in some areas of Malawi. Moreover a possible estrangement of children from Muslim families was to be avoided. Additionally the following animals from the OHP were exchanged: a ladybird, a deer, an owl, a hedgehog, a snail. They were replaced with a beetle, a goat, a bird, a mouse and a snake. In the picture-stories two changes were made: In the second story the girl in the Malawian version is eating a banana instead of ice cream. The fourth story involves two cyclists, while the original uses scooter as its mode of transport.

Summary

Using a slightly changed standardised test proved to be no problem. During the test it became apparent that Malawian children in rural areas rarely came into contact with picture material. At the beginning of the test phase they were very shy, but they slowly became accustomed to the material. The tests started with a few questions in order to dissolve the pupils' fears. Here the linguistic and writing environment within the family was of interest. In their mother tongue, the research assistants explained in a sympathetic calm voice, that the pupil will be shown a few pictures and should answer questions about these. The pupils were encouraged to hold the material in their hands in order to familiarise themselves with it. Most pupils felt free when handling the cards, yet some remained very shy until the end and stared at the test-supervisor with wide eyes when they were given the solution.

3.1.2. The interview as an instrument of data collection

For a differentiated and comprehensive description of personal opinions and positions, qualitative interviews seemed the most fitting instrument. They offer genuine and extensive information and gather facts, knowledge, opinions, positions or values (Schnell et al. 2005:325 ff.).

In order to gather prevailing views on the mental development and learning of Malawian primary school pupils, semi-structured face-to-face individual interviews with mostly open questions were conducted.[32] Open questions were posed in order to give the interviewee the opportunity to voice their views freely, without prerequisites or offered alternatives, which they had not taken into account prior to this. Here differences in the ability of expression could lead to more differentiated answers, while opinions on a topic and perceptions were possibly similar.

After finalising the interview guidelines, they were tested at various levels before going into the field. After discussions with colleagues from the University of Malawi, interviews were conducted at the District Education Office in Zomba. These steps proved to be very helpful. It showed that some of the questions were too complicated or too long and that the sequence required changes. These pre-interviews examined the variations of the answers, the plausibility of the questions, and the interest of the interviewee towards the questions as well as the duration of the interview.

The interviews were partly conducted in the indigenous languages aided by translations of the research assistants or the teacher. The translations slightly changed the questions at times, for instance if the translator's experience fed into the question or if replacement vocabulary was used. In order to avoid these changes, the questions were formulated in a very simple manner without technical terms, and the translator was briefed before the interview.

Village inhabitants, teachers, teacher-trainers and staff of the Malawian Ministry of Education were interviewed. Besides the general questions on the views and the meaning of instruction in the mother tongue, descriptions of logical thinking and the importance of the formal schooling system[33] were questioned. When formulating the questions, the professional and personal background of the interviewee was taken into account and four different interview guidelines were used[34].

Interviews with the teachers

The interviews with the teachers were the most comprehensive, as the lesson design was questioned in detail. The first section focused on the teacher's mother tongue and the role it plays during lessons and in relation to the mental development of the pupils. In the second section, the specific lesson atmosphere and design were of interest. The teacher was asked about his or her means of promoting logical thinking, his or her preferences and arguments for using specific exercises, dealing with above average and below average pupils, as well

[32] Variations of interview forms can be found in Konrad 2005, Schnell et al. 2005:322 amongst others.

[33] Characterization of formal, non-formal and informal education in 2.4.6.

[34] See Appendix 2 to 5.

as the language in which the pupils communicate with one another and with the teacher.

Interviews with the teacher-trainers
In the interviews with teacher-trainers, a special emphasis was laid on the theoretical knowledge of cognitive development in children and available instruction methods. The trainer's own teaching style at the Teacher Training Colleges was also of interest. The teacher-trainers were asked about their stance on instruction in the mother tongue and about ways to motivate logical thinking amongst the pupils.

Interviews with the village community
Some parents of the tested pupils as well as village elders from the primary schools' sphere of influence were called upon to voice their opinion on instruction in the mother tongue and its advantages and disadvantages. The backing and the support of the population are important if changes are introduced.

Interviews with Ministry of Education staff
The interviews with the District Education Officers, the Primary Education Advisors and Education Methods Advisory Section Officers included twelve questions. Among other questions, they were asked about their definition and views of instruction in the mother tongue, as well as the development of mental structures in school. They also voiced their opinion about the feasibility of instruction in the mother tongue in a multilingual society such as Malawi.

3.2. Research authorisation and ethical questions

Prior to the data collection an authorisation from the Ministry of Education was obtained in order to uphold the required ethical standards. There was a close collaboration with the District Education Officers as well as the respective Primary Education Advisors in the three research districts. The Malawi Institute of Education was informed about the study and offered their assistance.

All persons involved, were informed about the general aim of the study, but not about the underlying hypothesis. They were briefed about what would happen during the test and what their specific task would involve. All participants received the same instructions and were asked whether they understood what was expected of them. The participation in the study was without exception of a voluntary nature. The names of the interviewees were discarded after the contact was made and they were reassured that their statements would be treated with discretion and would not be passed on to third parties.

The pupils of the pilot and control classes were participants in the three year pilot project and were therefore aware of the content and its meaning. They agreed to participate.

3.3. Research areas and the sample population

One of the first steps of a study is a careful selection of the sample population, so that study insights would characterise the general public (Schnell et al. 2005:267 ff.).

Pupils from the "Literacy across the curriculum" (LAC) pilot project were selected to study the effects of the language of instruction in the early primary school years on mental development.[35] The tests were conducted in three regions of Malawi, in rural schools near Rumphi of the Citumbuka speaking area in the north, in rural schools near Mangochi in the south-east Ciyawo speaking area and as a control, in central Malawi's Ntcheu District. In the central region the predominant language is the national language Chichewa, which is the medium of instruction in Malawian schools since 1968. The Chichewa speaking pupils were taught in their mother tongue, just as their counterparts in the control classes in the Ciyawo and Citumbuka speaking areas. They were, however, evaluated separately, as there were no pilot and control pupils in this study and all pupils were taught in their mother tongue. The difference in the lessons merely came to pass through the learner-centred approach in the pilot schools. From the 18 pilot schools of the LAC project, two pilot schools respectively in the Ciyawo, Citumbuka and Chichewa speaking areas were selected at random and 125 pupils were taken into the sample population. Additionally, 125 pupils from the six LAC control schools in these regions were tested.

The characteristic differences between the pilot and control groups were presented in detail in the first chapter (2.5.1.) and table 3.1. acts as a reminder.

	Pilot class	**Control class**
Medium of Instruction	Language of the area (Ciyawo or Citumbuka)	Chichewa
Methodology	Learner-centred using group work, boss system[36]; Reading through writing	Teacher-centred
Teaching and learning material	Translated into language of the area; additional material developed by teachers	Already available materials

Table 3.1.Characteristics of pilot and control classes (Langer 2010:76)

The advantage of testing participants of a pre-existing study is that the testing could start immediately and time intensive and costly selection processes were avoided. The study participants were selected from the general population at the start of the project with regards to specific criteria (MIE 2003:3 f.). The selec-

[35] More information on this project in 2.5.1.

[36] Details in 3.6.2. (Evaluation of teacher interviews)

tion of these pupils for the presented study was based on the assumption that the pupils represent the general public and the sample results can be generalised.

The first tests were conducted in November 2006 in rural schools around Mangochi and were extended to Rumphi in the north and Ntcheu in the central region in March 2007. As mentioned earlier on, the predominant language in Mangochi is Ciyawo, in Rumphi Citumbuka and in Ntcheu the national language Chichewa.

The Ciyawo and Citumbuka speaking pilot pupils were exclusively instructed in the mother tongue during their first three years of primary school. They started learning English and Chichewa in Standard 3 and were then taught in a trilingual school system. The pupils in the central region, whose mother tongue is Chichewa, started learning English as their second language in Standard 3.

The selection of the test persons for the first research phase in Mangochi was not entirely unproblematic. As 11 individual tests were to be performed, every ninth pupil in the class register of 109 pupils who were marked as present was called up. However, not all registered children were actually present. Some children were ill, others had dropped out of school or were repeating Standard 3 or they had transferred to another school. If the ninth pupil was absent, the tenth pupil was called in order to guarantee a certain degree of random selection. In some schools, pupils were registered as present without actually being there.

The tests were conducted in the schools as indicated in table 3.2.

Pilot school	Control school	Mother tongue of the pupils	Total of pupils		Test date
			Girls	Boys	
1st Test phase					
	Kasolo	Ciyawo	6	5	8th /9th Nov. 2006
Chimbende		Ciyawo	7	6	10th /11th Nov. 2006
	Ndengu	Ciyawo	8	6	13th /14th Nov. 2006
Mtuwa		Ciyawo	4	8	15th /16th Nov. 2006
2nd Test phase					
	Chozoli	Citumbuka	14	11	12th /13th March 2007
Chombe		Citumbuka	14	12	14th /15th March 2007
	Mkombezi	Citumbuka	13	11	16th /17th March 2007
Ng'onga		Citumbuka	12	13	19th /20th March 2007
Chiole		Chichewa	13	12	22nd /23rd March 2007
	Dombole	Chichewa	11	14	24th /26th March 2007
	Bangala	Chichewa	14	11	27th /28th March 2007
Chilobwe		Chichewa	12	13	29th /30th March 2007

Table 3.2. Test phase (Langer 2010:77)

In Rumphi and Ntcheu, a different approach was taken. Names were called up in reference to a list of pupils who sat for the last LAC test. However even here, only 116 of 160 LAC tested pupils were present. Consequently further pupils were called up from the class register according to the principle of random selection.

3.4. Research assistants

This study was designed for Standard four pupils in Malawian rural areas, which is why the help of assistants who were conversant in the local language was indispensible. In the new test situation the pupils were supposed to experience a familiar element, the mother tongue.

Following some research at the University of Malawi's Centre for Educational Research and Training (CERT), the first assistant, Ms. Bessie Chirwa, was introduced to the study. She helped with the translation of the tests into Ciyawo, probed the usefulness of the original tests and its adequacy in the Malawian context. She also assisted during the testing phase in Mangochi. Mrs. Catherine Mwanachawa and Mrs. Linda Bwanali helped with the Citumbuka and Chichewa translation as well as conducting the second test phase. During the second test phase more pupils were tested, due to the fact that the GTZ kindly funded a great portion of the budget.

During the collaboration a few smaller problems arose. When working with an assistant, a comprehensive sensitisation is very important to ensure the confident handling of the research tools. The use of quantitative methods does not allow for individual attention and must guarantee the same conditions for all participants (Rogge 1995:149). To achieve this, a trial-run was conducted with children in Zomba prior to the start of the respective test phase. This served the purpose of familiarising the assistants with the test material and the situation, rather than attaining actual results.

3.5. Time frame

When the study was conducted, the pilot project "Literacy across the Curriculum" had just finished with the end of the school year and was being evaluated. The test series fit into the existing discussions about the education language policy and hoped to complement the LAC results, highlighting further aspects of the possible influence of the language of instruction in early primary school years. The results of the study hoped to demonstrate whether there is a relationship between the development of selected elementary cognitive abilities and the language of instruction.

The Malawian school year is divided into three terms, which end with a three or four week holiday. The school year at the time of the study started in January and ended in November. Because the first tests could only be conducted just before the start of the holidays in November 2006, the test series was divided in two different periods. The second test series took place in March 2007. The interruption was not optimal, but unavoidable due to financial and organisational restrictions.

3.6. Data analysis

In the following section the test and interviews are evaluated and the results are displayed.

3.6.1. The test

In the statistical analysis of the test, the presented results were first examined using descriptive statistics. Subsequently conclusions from individual cases into general statements were made through inductive statistics.

The terms *variable* or *unit* will repeatedly appear in the text and have the same meaning. Prior to the investigation, the to-be examined properties will be named “units with their associated characteristics”, while they will be called “variables as characteristics of units” during data collection and analysis. In the presented study, variables with which no further statistical calculations were to be conducted, such as gender, school type, questions on the home and school environment, were scaled nominally. Most of the measured units of collected data were displayed on an interval scaling level, as different mathematical calculations were supposed to be conducted with them. This concerns dependent variables, which obtained varying results due to the manipulation of independent variables (Kranz 1997:9 ff.). In this study these are for instance the marks obtained in the individual exercises in the different schools. At the end of the statistical analysis these were converted into percentages in order to make them comparable.

The computer programme SPSS[37] was used for the analysis of quantitative data. SPSS is frequently used in the social sciences for administrative purposes and the statistical analysis of data. The data is coded and the code lists of the study are attached (Appendix 6 to 9).

The tests were conducted in two phases and the first results were obtained in November 2006 in the Ciyawo speaking area. During the analysis of this first data set, the aim was to identify the first tendencies and indications for the validation or the annulment of the hypothesis. In December preliminary results were presented during a language symposium in Malawi. The focus of the twenty minute presentation looked at the comparison of the results for the control and the pilot classes. In the analysis of the sample group the aim was to generalise the results and draw general conclusions from the collected data. With the help of the level of significance, conclusions about the general significance or probability of doubt could be drawn. Table 3.3. demonstrates that the

[37] Statistical Products and Service Solution (originally Statistical Package for the Social Sciences).

average marks of the pupils from the pilot and the control class from the Ciyawo speaking area showed a high deviance in the OHP subtest as well as in the RA subtest on the 5 percent level. As the differences of the sample group were not significant in every case, the results could have occurred by chance and a repetition of the test might show different results.

School type & points	**N**	**Significance α**	
Task OHP	50	0,006	significant at 1% niveau
Task GF	50	0,150	not significant
Task RF	50	0,671	not significant
Task RA	50	0,049	significant at 5% niveau

Table 3.3. Differences in the average marks of the four exercises between the pilot and control groups in the Ciyawo speaking area. (Langer 2010:80)

In March 2007, the data of the two other language areas was collected.

Descriptive statistics
Descriptive statistics as a depiction of the sample population of 250 pupils, illustrate the results in the form of tables, diagrams and overviews.

At first, a frequency distribution of all the collated variables is carried out (Schnell et al. 2005:441). The *absolute frequency* helps to demonstrate how often certain units, especially the nominally scaled variables, appear. The conversion into the *percentile frequency* allows the comparison of the results with other similar studies. In the presented study the sample population of the different language groups varies in size. 50 Ciyawo mother tongue speakers were tested, while 100 mother tongue speakers of Citumbuka and Chichewa were tested respectively. With the aid of the percentile frequency it is possible to compare all the obtained results. In metrically scaled variables the number of the observable characteristic occurrence is generally very high and such a frequency distribution would be too chaotic. In order to obtain a more meaningful distribution of the interval scaled characteristics, these are transformed into ordinal scaled variables. An example from the presented study is the age indication. Pupil age groups were formed with "1" represented 7 to 9 years; "2": 10 to 12 year olds; "3": 13 years and older.

Subsequently, the mean value of the control and pilot group was calculated from the different exercises and compared.

To question of which correlations exist between metrically scaled variables and how strong the correlation is, can be calculated through the *correlation coefficient*. This produces a value between + / - 1 and where the correlation is stronger, the coefficient is close to + / - 1. The result of +1 characterises a unidirectional or a perfect positive correlation and means that an increase of the one variable would also cause an increase in the other. Therefore, if a pupil attains a high value in one variable, it is very probable that he/she will also attain a high value in the other variable. A coefficient near -1 on the other hand means that an increase in one variable results in a decrease of another. The presented study uses *Pearson*'s method to calculate the correlation coefficient.

The correlation between discrete variables is shown in *cross-classified tables;* between the metrically scaled variables in *mean value tables*.

Gender distribution in the pilot and control groups

128 girls were tested and 122 boys, and respectively 61 girls and 64 boys in the six pilot schools and 67 girls and 58 boys in the control schools.

Age distribution in the pilot and control groups

The age group distribution was similar in the pilot and control groups. 66 percent of the tested pupils were between 10 and 12 years of age and therefore slightly older than Standard 3 or 4 pupils in Germany.

Age rate	**Pilot pupils (n=125)**	**Control pupils (n=125)**	**Total**
7-9 years	26,4%	20,0%	23,2%
10-12 years	63,2%	68,0%	65,6%
13 years and older	10,4%	12,0%	11,2%

Table 3.4. Age distribution in the pilot and control groups (Langer 2010:82)

Language and gender distribution in the pilot and control groups

100 pupils were tested in the Chichewa speaking region, 50 from pilot schools and 50 from control schools. From the pilot schools and the control schools, 25 girls and 25 boys were tested respectively. In Mangochi, the Ciyawo speaking area, 50 children were tested; amongst these were 11 girls and 14 boys from pilot schools as well as 14 girls and 11 boys from control schools. In the North, 100 Citumbuka mother tongue speakers were tested, 25 girls and 25 boys from the pilot school as well as 28 girls and 22 boys from the control schools.

Literacy levels of the parents in the pilot and control groups

Both in the control and in the pilot schools, most pupils indicated that both their parents can read. If the numbers are divided into language groups, it became apparent that in the Chichewa and Citumbuka speaking areas, the number of literate parents of the pilot pupils was higher than of the control group. The Ciyawo region displayed a different scenario. Here 60 percent of the parents of the control pupils were literate while only 44 percent of the parents of the pilot group were literate. Generally speaking it should be noted that the literacy level of both parents in a sample population in the Ciyawo speaking area showed the

Literacy level	Pilot pupils (n=125)	Control pupils (n=125)	Total
Both parents	70,4%	62,4%	66,4%
One parent	8,0%	5,6%	6,8%
No parent	21,6%	32,0%	26,8%

Table 3.5. Literacy level of the parents (Langer 2010:82)

lowest literacy level with only 52 percent. Within the sample group of parents in the Citumbuka speaking area, 61 percent were literate and 79 percent in the sample group of the tested Chichewa speakers were literate.

The Chi² test showed a significance level of 0,002 which means that the result reflects the general population and was therefore not coincidental.

Parents reading to the children in pilot and control group homes

Building up on the question about the parents' literacy, the pupils were asked if the parents read to them. In thc families of the 125 tested pilot pupils, 69 percent of the parents regularly read to the children. Of the 125 control pupil families only 46 percent did the same. The reason for this could be that the parents of the pilot pupils were reminded and aware of academically relevant topics and supported their children in the learning process. If one looks at the different language groups, the difference within the Citumbuka speaking group is very distinctive. 64 percent of the parents of the pilot pupils read to them regularly, but only 26 percent of the parents of the control group did this. It was queried whether the pupils come into contact with reading and writing outside school.

Ability to write one's own name

Nearly half of the control pupils were able to write their own name and family name, however 41 of the 125 tested pupils i.e. a third, were unable to do this. Only 9 pupils managed to write a whole correct sentence. The pilot pupils presented a very different picture. 71 pupils could write their name correctly in a full sentence, while 8 pupils could not write their first and surname at all.

This result reflected the LAC test results. The aim of the pilot study was to promote reading, writing and mathematical abilities. The conclusive tests at the end of that study, displayed a very distinctive difference between the pilot and control pupils.[38]

[38] More detailed information on the LAC pilot project in Chapter 2.

Ability to write one's own name	Pilot pupils (n=125)	Control pupils (n=125)	Total
In a correct sentence[39]	56,8%	7,2%	32,0%
With mistakes in a sentence	16,0%	14,4%	15,2%
Only name	20,8%	45,6%	33,2%
Nothing	6,4%	32,8%	19,6%

Table 3.6. Ability to writes one's own name (Langer 2010:83)

Results of the subtests, divided into language and school type:
The following tables show the means of the different BIVA subtests. In the first table, the results of the Ciyawo and Citumbuka groups are displayed and in the second table the results are compared with the Chichewa speakers. Beside the teaching approach, the pilot and control groups of the Ciyawo and Citumbuka speakers differ mainly in the language of instruction.

A) Results of the subtest isolating objects, positive
In the subtest *isolating objects, positive*, the average of all participating pilot

	Mean value		Significance α
	Pilot pupils	Control pupils	
Ciyawo-Speaker (N=50 pupils)	96,4%	90,4%	0,01
Citumbuka-Speaker (N=100 pupils)	96,0%	95,0%	0,53
Total– Ciyawo- and Citumbuka-Speaker (N=150 pupils)	96,2%	93,5%	0,04
Chichewa-Speaker (N=100 pupils)	97,4%	97,8%	0,70

Table 3.7. Percentage on average, subtest *isolating objects, positive*, divided into pilot and control pupils of the language areas (Langer 2010:84)

pupils was 96.2 percent of the possible 18 points. In the individual language group sample, the following could be observed: The Ciyawo pilot pupils reached an average of 96.4 percent and the Citumbuka pilot pupils attained 96.0 percent. If these results are compared to the control group, a high discrepancy between the pilot pupils (96.4 percent) and the control pupils (90.4) is visible. If the

[39] Ciyawo: "Lina lyangu ndi(ne) … ."
Citumbuka: "Zina lane ndi(ne) … ."
Chichewa: "Dzina langa ndi(ne) … ."

results are compared to the Chichewa speaking pilot pupils, it is apparent that with 97.4 percent of the possible number of points, these pupils showed a slightly better performance.

B) Results of the subtest pictoral stories

In the second subtest, *pictoral stories*, the Ciyawo speakers, especially the control pupils, who reached 69.3 percent of the possible 18 points, attained very high marks in comparison to the Citumbuka speakers. As this result had a high deviance from the others, it is to be treated with caution.

Due to a significance of 0.84 and 0.15 the results of both the Ciyawo and Citumbuka speaking groups could be coincidental. In the Chichewa speaking group the control pupils also attained very high marks.

	Mean value		Significance α
	Pilot pupils	Control pupils	
Ciyawo-Speaker (N=50 pupils)	61,3%	69,3%	0,84
Citumbuka-Speaker (N=100 pupils)	59,8%	54,7%	0,15
Total – Ciyawo- and Citumbuka-Speaker (N=150 pupils)	60,28%	59,6%	0,28
Chichewa-Speaker (N=100 pupils)	65,6%	72,8%	0,08

Table 3.8. Percentage on average, subtest *pictoral stories*, divided into pilot and control pupils of the three language areas (Langer 2010:85)

C) Results of the subtest continuing sequence

	Mean value		Significance α
	Pilot pupils	Control pupils	
Ciyawo-Speaker (N=50 pupils)	73,1%	70,4%	0,67
Citumbuka-Speaker (N=100 pupils)	73,1%	63,4%	0,04
Total – Ciyawo- and Citumbuka-Speaker (N=150 pupils)	73,1%	65,8%	0,05
Chichewa-Speaker (N=100 pupils)	69,6%	72,9%	0,49

Table 3.9. Percentage on average, subtest *continuing sequence*, divided into pilot and control pupils of the three language areas (Langer 2010:86)

In the subtest *continuing sequence*, the average mark of the pilot pupils of both language groups was the same. Amongst the control pupils, the Ciyawo speakers attained higher points than the Citumbuka speakers. The difference between the pilot and control group of both language groups nearly amounted to 10 percent. The pilot pupils performed better than the pilot and control pupils of the Chichewa speaking group, who attained less than 73 percent in this exercise.

D) Results of the subtest analogy sequence
The analysis of the results of the fourth test, *analogy sequence*, demonstrated that the Citumbuka speakers had much better results than the Ciyawo speakers and reached higher marks. The difference between the pilot and the control pupils within the Ciyawo speaking group was higher by over 10 percent and the result lay within the level of significance of 0.05. The Chichewa speakers solved the problem better and attained higher marks than the pupils of the other language groups.

	Mean value		**Significance α**
	Pilot pupils	**Control pupils**	
Ciyawo-Speaker (N=50 pupils)	68,0%	55,8%	0,03
Citumbuka-Speaker (N=100 pupils)	74,3%	70,4%	0,05
Total – Ciyawo- and Citumbuka-Speaker (N=150 pupils)	72,2%	65,6%	0,70
Chichewa-Speaker (N=100 pupils)	75,6%	76,6%	0,77

Table 3.10. Percentage on average, subtest *analogy sequence,* divided into pilot and control pupils of the three language areas (Langer 2010:86)

E) Sum of the results of the four subtests
When summing up the results of the four tests, a general advantage of the pilot pupils over the control pupils could be observed in the Ciyawo and Citumbuka speaking areas. With a few exceptions, the Ciyawo and Citumbuka speaking pilot pupils achieved higher marks than the pupils of the control classes.

The results of the intelligence test showed that the pupils who were taught in their mother tongue in their first three years of school, performed better at solving the problems. They demonstrated better thinking abilities in respect to the three sub-processes of conclusive thinking – isolation, comparison, and transferral. The Chichewa mother tongue speakers were slightly better at solving the problems, by 77 percent in the pilot classes and 80 percent in the control classes. The teaching approach was the only distinguishing factor here. It is noticeable that the pilot Ciyawo and Citumbuka speaking pupils – who were taught in a familiar language – attained nearly the same number of points in the analysis of the development level of selected elementary cognitive operations as the Chichewa speakers. They developed their conclusive thinking abilities in a similar manner as the Chichewa speakers and very differently from the control pupils of the Ciyawo and Citumbuka test population, who received the conventional instruction in Chichewa.

	Mean value		**Significance α**
	Pilot pupils	**Control pupils**	
Ciyawo-Speaker (N=50 pupils)	74,7%	71,5%	0,03
Citumbuka-Speaker (N=100 pupils)	75,8%	70,9%	0,37
Total – Ciyawo- and Citumbuka-Speaker (N=150 pupils)	75,4%	71,1%	0,04
Chichewa-Speaker (N=100 pupils)	77,0%	80,0%	0,2

Table 3.11. Sum of all subtests, divided into pilot and control pupils of the three language areas (Langer 2010:87)

Inductive statistics

The validity of the obtained results for the general population was subsequently tested (*inductive statistics*). Of interest was whether the results of the sample population were transferrable to the general population as well as whether the hypotheses could be confirmed or rejected. In this way it could be ensured that the differences between the groups were not simply coincidental (Schnell et al. 2005:60 ff.). The probability of error was set at 95 percent[40]. This means that there is a 5 percent probability that the result of the sample is false or cannot be applied to the general population. In the social sciences, a level of significance of 0.01 and 0.05[41] is usual (Fröhlich et al. 2005).

There are several testing methods within inductive statistics which are used depending on the scales of measure. The methods used in the presented study, the *chi² test,* the *independent t-test,* the *variance analysis* and the *correlation coefficient* are presented below.

The *chi² test* examines whether there is a dependence between the variables in a cross tabulation. The result is obtained from the deviance of the observed factors from the expected, to decide whether the examined variables display a dependency (Schnell et al. 2005:449 f.) and the hypothesis is confirmed or disregarded.

---

[40] Equivalent to the level of significance of 0.05.

[41] Meaning: Significance of a 1 percent or 5 percent level.

Correlation between ability to write one's own name in a correct sentence and a literate environment
Pupils from homes in which books are present were often able to write their name in a correct sentence. The chi² test displayed a result of 9.263 with 3 degrees of freedom[42] and a significance value of 0.026. The test confirmed that a literate environment supports the literacy of the children.

Correlation between the ability to write one's name in a correct sentence and the language background
It was queried whether the ability to write one's own name depended on the mother tongue of the tested children or their cultural background. The Chi² showed a highly significant correlation on the one percent level with a value of 25.345 and 6 degrees of freedom. The result indicates, that cultural differences concerning the acceptance and meaning of reading and writing abilities exist.

Correlation between the ability to write one's own name in a correct sentence and the school type (pilot and control school)
At the one percent level, there is a highly significant correlation between the ability to write one's own name and the school type (pilot or control school).The chi² test displayed a value of 81.985 with 3 degrees of freedom. The tests showed that most pupils who participated in the LAC pilot project in their first three years of school were able to write their name in a correct full sentence.

The *independent t-test* compares the arithmetic middle of the metrical variable in the two different groups (Fröhlich et al. 2005) and is a means to verify the applicability of the sample group to the general population. For this, the independent variable must be dichotomous, meaning that it has exactly two characteristic traits and the dependent variable must be metrically scaled. As an example of a t-test, the following tables compare the performance of the control and pilot pupils in the different subtests.

Significance test between the control and pilot group in the first test, divided into language groups
The following table presents the results of the independent t-test, showing significant differences between the pilot and control schools in the first subtest in the different language areas.

The results of the pilot and control pupils in the Ciyawo speaking area in the first subtest show significant differences at the one percent level. These different results of the pilot and control pupils are relevant to the general population with a probability of 99 percent.

[42] Degrees of freedom = Number of undetermined values which make up a statistic (for instance the average value). The more degrees of freedom a statistic has, the more statistically significant the actual group differences are.

It is possible that the differences between the pilot and control groups of the Citumbuka and Chichewa speakers was coincidental and that a repeated test with a different sample group would attain different results.

Subtest	Ciyawo	Citumbuka	Chichewa
OHP	0,006	0,533	0,703

Table 3.12. Significance test between the control and pilot group in the first test, divided into language groups. (Langer 2010:89)

Significance test between the control and pilot groups in the second and third test, divided into language groups

The independent t-test showed a significant difference in dealing with the tasks for the three language groups in the second and third subtest above the five percent level. The results could be coincidental and are probably not relevant for the general population.

Subtest	Ciyawo	Citumbuka	Chichewa
GF	0,150	0,283	0,08
RF	0,671	0,390	0,492

Table 3.13. Significance test between the control and pilot group in the second and third, divided into language groups. (Langer 2010:90)

Significance test between the control and pilot group in the fourth test, divided into language groups

In the Ciyawo speaking region, the results of the pilot and control groups in the fourth subtest deviated significantly at the five percent level. These different results of the pilot and control pupils show a 95 percent relevance for the general population. The different test results of the Citumbuka as well as the Chichewa speakers could be coincidental and repeated tests with a different sample population could attain different results.

Subtest	Ciyawo	Citumbuka	Chichewa
RA	0,049	0,700	0,765

Table 3.14. Significance test between the control and pilot group in the fourth, divided into language groups (Langer 2010:90)

Results of the significance test between the pilot and control group, Ciyawo and Citumbuka combined

The following table shows the level of significance on which the point average values of the pilot and control groups differ. The examined results encompass the pilot and control groups from the Ciyawo and Citumbuka speaking regions. This evaluation made the possible influence of the use of a familiar language instead of an unfamiliar language during the first few years of school more visible, as three of the four subtests showed significant differences in the handling of the tasks.

Subtest	Significance
OHP	0,040
GF	0,842
RF	0,050
RA	0,030

Table 3.15. Results of the significance test between the control and pilot group of the entire sample population (Langer 2010:91)

The combined results of the two language groups show that the differences between the pilot and control groups give a valid and not a coincidental reflection of the general population. The better results of the pilot pupils in the first, third and fourth tests can be transferred to the general population. The results of the second subtest form a noticeable exception with significance at a ten percent level. According to the independent t-test, the results of the second subtest, *pictoral story*, could be coincidental and cannot be transferred to the general population. It became apparent that the use of the children's mother tongue in the pilot classes, improved their test results.

The *variance analysis*[43] or the *unifactorial ANOVA,* tests whether the mean values of any number of groups display a significant difference within the group. In contrast to the t-test, this method is used for the polytomous independent and metrically scaled dependent variables. *Polytomous variables* are variables with more than two characteristics. The variable "ability to write name" for instance contains four characteristics, being "no", "only the name", "whole sentence with errors" and "correct sentence". In our study, the existence of a significant difference between the results of the individual tasks and the ability to write one's own name in a correct sentence was tested with the help of the variance analysis.

Conclusions from the results of the individual tasks in respect to the ability to write one's own name in a correct sentence

The analysis concluded that it is not possible to relate the results of the subtests to the ability to write one's name in a correct sentence. One can therefore not

[43] Variance characterises the distribution of the measured values around the arithmetic middle.

assume that a pupil who is good at solving the problems also shows good reading and writing skills.

The relationship between the metrically scaled variables was examined with the help of the correlation coefficient, which may show a value between +/- 1. In order to answer the question, whether the found correlation also exists in the general population, the t-value (not be confused with the t-test) is calculated with the help of this coefficient, which is then compared to the critical value in a t-distribution and can then make conclusions about the possible coincidence of the result.

Subtest	F-Value	Degrees of freedom	Significance
OHP	1,215	3	0,306
GF	0,980	3	0,404
RF	0,980	3	0,404
RA	1,551	3	0,204

Table 3.16. Conclusions on the ability to write one's name in a correct full sentence in connection with school type. (Langer 2010:92)

Correlation between the achieved marks and the required time

With an increased complexity of the tests, the negative correlation between the achieved marks and the required time became apparent. This means that a pupil with higher marks required less time. The fourth test (*analogy series*) required the highest mental performance through the analogue transferral of the relationship in one order to another. The Pearson correlation coefficient amounted to – 0.618.

This relationship clarifies the "principal of simplification", which according to Klix (1983) defines a higher degree of intelligence through a lower mental effort.

Relationship between points and required time	Correlation coefficient	Significance
Subtest OHP	-0,381	0,01
Subtest GF	-0,327	0,01
Subtest RF	-0,390	0,01
Subtest RA	-0,618	0,01

Table 3.17. Relationship between the attained points and the required time (Langer 2010:93)

In the following tables the relationship between the achieved points and the required time is divided into pilot and control groups.

In the pilot groups, a negative correlation between the achieved number of test points and the time required to find a solution can be observed. This negative correlation increases with the complexity of the problem. In the more complex tasks of the subtest series analogy, the correlation coefficient amounted to -0.578 in contrast to -0.307 between the more simple first test (isolating the object, positive) and the required time.

Relationship between points and required time in the pilot group	Correlation coefficient	Significance
Subtest OHP	-0,307	0,01
Subtest GF	-0,403	0,01
Subtest RF	-0,403	0,01
Subtest RA	-0,578	0,01

Table 3.18. Relationship between the achieved points and the required time in the pilot group (Langer 2010:93)

The correlation between the marks and the required time is also negative for the control group and is highest for the most difficult task (series analogy). For the second task, the correlation value amounts to -0.293. This means that there is a little relationship between the achieved marks and the required time.

Relationship between points and required time in the control group	Correlation coefficient	Significance
Subtest OHP	-0,606	0,01
Subtest GF	-0,293	0,01
Subtest RF	-0,491	0,01
Subtest RA	-0,668	0,01

Table 3.19. Relationship between the achieved points and the required time in the control group (Langer 2010:94)

Summary of the test results

The pupils who were instructed in a familiar language during their early primary school years achieved better results in the BIVA test. These results support the hypothesis that the use of a familiar language promotes the mental abilities and the psychological development of the currently disadvantaged Ciyawo and Citumbuka speaking pupils. The pupils from the pilot groups who were exclusively instructed in a familiar language during the first three years of school, showed the same level of development as the Chichewa speaking comparison group. As explained above, Chichewa has been the national language for over 40 years and enjoys a very high status. Historically, other local languages were suppressed or disregarded. Through the use of the local languages at school the self-esteem of the pupils raises. The speakers of the language feel recognised and enjoy going to school.

In the presented study there were hardly any differences between the results of the pilot pupils and the Chichewa speakers. They solved the problems slightly better than the Ciyawo and Citumbuka speakers. If the results of the pilot and control groups of the latter two language groups are compared, a clear difference is visible. During the exercises, the pilot pupils nearly caught up with the Chichewa speakers and were nearly as apt as their counterparts in solving the problems.

The test population can be divided into four groups, the Chichewa speaking pilot and control group (with the teaching approach as the divisive characteristic) and the Ciyawo and Citumbuka speaking pilot and control group (with the teaching approach and the language of instruction as the divisive characteristic). Due to the fact that the Chichewa speaking control pupils achieved better tests results than the pilot pupils it can be concluded that the teaching approach had a lower influence on the development of conclusive thinking abilities than the language of instruction. The tested pupils participated in the LAC pilot project from 2004 until the end of 2006. At the start of the pilot project, the participants were carefully selected from the general population. Factors such as the command of language, age, gender, support and interest of the community were decisive; language of the school environment, access to the school throughout the year as well as the comparative facilities of the schools (MIE 2003:3 f.) also played a role. The selection of these pupils for the presented study was based on the assumption, that the pupils are representative of the general population and that the results would be relevant for all Malawian primary school pupils.

Finally, it can be said that the development of pupils from different language groups is supported through instruction in the mother tongue and that possible disadvantages can be countered.

3.6.2. Interviews

The main objective of the data processing is the structuring and reduction (Rogge 1995:186). The aim is to create an overview of the "vast amounts of related, but confusing information" in order to structure it (Rogge 1995:186). While details are minimised, important information is accentuated in order to present the relevant characteristics of the original data (Woods et al. 1986:8). With the help of different forms of presentation such as tables, lists and diagrams the relevant information is displayed.

The results from closed written interviews can easily be translated into numerical values through indications and scaling in the questionnaire (Rogge 1995:104). The evaluation was more comprehensive due to the fact that the interviews were conducted in an open verbal fashion (Schnell et al. 2005:332). The answers from the verbal interviews were categorised and summarised thematically. With the aid of these categories, the answers were comparable. If an answer did not fit into the previously defined category, a new category was inductively established out of specific material, paying attention to separation specificity, unambiguity, sufficiency and economics. The collated answers were isolated and subdivided under specific headings. All answers which were relevant to the study were noted and no more categories were established than necessary (Rogge 1995:187).

After the categorisation the data was fed into a data matrix. Similarly to the test evaluation, the type of data scaling determines the possible methodology used for the analysis of the interviews.

In contrast to quantitative research in which "an instrument that is independent from the context und the persons collecting the data, shows identical data for the same person" (Helfferich 2005:138), qualitative interviews are always context dependent and cannot give identical answers when repeatedly asked.

Qualitative research occurs in the natural environment of the interviewee and aims to "address specific social problems, do research for the affected persons and wants to create an open, balanced interview situation" (Mayring 2002:146).

Below, the interviews were divided and interpreted within the target groups and the most prominent answers were selected for discussion. The full interviews can be found in the appendix of the study.

The teachers

Teachers from 9 pilot, 9 control as well as 2 demonstrations schools were interviewed. Demonstration schools are attached to the governmental Teacher Training Colleges (TTCs) and follow the primary school curriculum in the same ways as other schools with the difference that they offer the teacher-students of the TTCs the opportunity to conduct lessons. In total 20 teachers were interviewed, 11 women and 9 men. Amongst the interview partners, six completed 10th grade (Junior Certificate of Education) and 14 teachers completed secondary education with the Malawi Secondary School Certificate of Education after 12 years of school.

8 of the interview partners were Chichewa mother tongue speakers, 2 Ciyawo, 9 Citumbuka and one Citonga mother tongue speakers.

Importance of the language of instruction

According to 19 of the 20 teachers, the use of a familiar language has the advantage that the children can follow the lessons more easily, gain a better understanding of the topics, can express their exact views on the matter and have a better basis of communication with the teacher. One teacher in the Ciyawo speaking region however, commented that she only uses Chichewa and English in the higher classes, as the school books and exams are set in these languages. Besides this, she did not know what influence the language of instruction could have on the lessons. All teachers indicated that the pupils always communicated in their mother tongue during group exercises and that the pupils felt more confident if they were allowed to contribute to the lessons in a familiar language. Moreover, 13 of the interviewed teachers claimed that the change of instruction in the mother tongue displayed a more active participation, as the pupils often found it difficult to express their views in a foreign language.

Learner-centred approaches and psychological development

15 teachers from the sample population want to promote their pupils' psychological development through the use of learner-centred approaches such as experiments, discussions and group work. 9 out of the 20 teachers claimed that own experiences of the pupils and prior knowledge are integrated into the subject matter. One teacher criticized the contents of Malawian curriculum are imported from other countries and that critical thinking and the question of the language of instruction are disregarded.

Logical thinking was defined as the ability to work in a critical and goal-oriented manner (9 teachers), to develop and express ideas (2 teachers) as well as the ability to transfer from a simple to a complex situation (4 teachers). 6 of the 20 teachers frequently use the so called "Boss system", in which one pupil plays the boss and has the answer and explains questions to his/her classmates. 13 teachers want to raise the pupils' mental performance by using various methods which utilise teaching aids from locally available materials, group work and role play. 8 of the interview partners addressed the abilities and weakness of their pupils. 13 of the interviewees challenged their pupils from time to time to test their prior knowledge and problem solving abilities by giving the pupils a new problem and motivating them to find their own solutions. Most of the teachers also use puzzles, fill-in-the-blanks texts and exercises in which the pupils have to arrange objects in a specific order. Generally speaking, 16 of the interviewed teachers claimed that their teaching methods promote thinking abilities and that a number of methods such as a systematic working approach, self control, supporting each other, foresighted thinking and problem solving abilities are developed.

Problems

One challenge which 12 of the interviewed teachers identified was the very different knowledge levels amongst the pupils, which they attributed to the frequent absence of pupils and the repetition of the classes. Another problem was the negative effect of having a large class in a poorly equipped classroom which lacked teaching material.

The teacher trainers

10 interviews were conducted with teacher trainers from four Teacher Training Colleges (TTCs). Four women and six men agreed to interviews, 8 of these had a University Diploma and one male as well as one female trainer had obtained a bachelor's degree. Four of the interview partners spoke Chichewa as their mother tongue, three Cilomwe, two Citumbuka and one trainer originated from Zimbabwe with Shona as the mother tongue.

Instruction in the mother tongue

When asked whether there was a difference between instruction in the mother tongue and in an unfamiliar language, all interview partners responded that an obvious difference existed. If the entire lesson was conducted in a familiar language, the pupils displayed a less inhibited participation in the lesson, expressed themselves more freely and could understand the teacher more easily. 9 out of the 10 trainers also indicated that the TTC pupils had fewer difficulties when learning in their mother tongue[44], were able to express themselves more clearly and therefore showed a more active and open participation in the classes. The trainers remarked that the pupils were more open, but sometimes had difficulties to express themselves correctly as the indigenous language lacked a number of technical terms. Moreover, the use of a familiar language had the effect that pupils were able to fully focus on the newly introduced concepts as there were no language barriers.

Learner-centred approaches and psychological development

With the help of pupil-centred teaching approaches, such as experiments, the pupils were able to build on existing knowledge and to develop a range of skills by learning through investigation. The psychological development of the children is apparently addressed in all subjects at the TTC and is a main focus of the subject Educational Foundation Studies. The trainers also tried to address aspects of psychological development in children in the appropriate lesson context. 4 trainers mentioned Bloom's taxonomy[45] as their basis, 5 trainers mentioned Piaget's practical approach[46]. By using a learner-centred approach, the trainers hoped to encourage the future teachers to self determined and autonomous learning, as well as offering them the opportunity to actively contribute to the lesson. They for instance, challenged their pupils by encouraging them to develop their own formulas from set examples and to demonstrate their creativity through the use of different materials.

[44] The language of instruction at the TTC is English.

[45] The process of dealing with the learnt material from simple (comparison, usage, analysis) to more complex (generation, evaluation) thinking abilities

[46] Learning from the specific to the abstract

The village community
39 interviews were conducted with village elders and parents of some of the tested pupils from pilot and control schools. The majority of the village elders in Malawian villages are men, a phenomenon which is also reflected in our study. Amongst the 19 interviewed village elders, 4 were female representatives and 15 were male. Furthermore 20 parents agreed to interviews, amongst them 11 mothers and 9 fathers.

The schools in which the tests were conducted are located in Malawi's rural areas and the fact that only 43 percent of the interviewed elders and parents had completed secondary or tertiary education is representative of the general population. One fifth of the interview partners indicated that they never attended school. The introduction of free primary education in 1994 enabled all children to attend school and the interview partners were not part of the target group of the political decision at that time. 15 Chichewa mother tongue speakers, 8 Ciyawo, 15 Citumbuka and one Bemba mother tongue speaker, living in a Citumbuka speaking area, were interviewed.

The group of 8 from the Ciyawo speaking area were much smaller than the groups from northern and central Malawi. However, it was indicative, that more than half of the group never received a formal education. In the Citumbuka and Chichewa speaking groups the percentage of interview partners who had not received a formal education was much lower and stood at 10 percent.

The representatives of the Ciyawo and Citumbuka speakers were raised in a multilingual environment, speaking their mother tongue in the home and village area and proudly passing this on to their children. However, they were forced to learn the national language Chichewa, as it plays a great role in their daily lives. Outside their own language area, Chichewa acts as the lingua franca and is also used as a means of communication in public institutions or with visitors. Very few books in Citumbuka and Ciyawo have found their way to the villages.

The language of instruction
To the question, in which language their children should be instructed in primary school, 56 percent from the Ciyawo and Citumbuka speaking sample population responded that they preferred instruction in the mother tongue in the early years of primary school and later in English. 24 percent of the group answered that they would prefer exclusive instruction in the mother tongue from Standard 1 to 8. 20 percent of the sample group swayed between a mix of the mother tongue and English in primary school (10 percent), a mix of Chichewa and English (8 percent) and an instruction exclusively in English from Standard 1 to 8 (2 percent).

Nearly 50 percent of the interview partners responded to the question of the importance of instruction in the mother tongue with the benefit of the pupils' improved understanding of taught concepts. 38 percent also noted the positive effect of maintaining the culture through the use of the indigenous language.

Instruction in the own language would create children who are proud to speak their language, who would be able to express themselves more clearly and would understand the concepts of the lessons. Choosing the mother tongue as a medium of instruction would also give the children an element of continuity in life. School enrolment would be less abrupt as the children would converse in the same language at home and during class. They would have fewer problems in speaking to their teachers and would attain better results, instead of being taught in a foreign language which would hinder their study.

Attitude towards formal education
95 percent of the interview partners described the formal education as a good preparation for life and the related search for employment, as well as the opportunity to overcome prejudices against one's own culture. The children learn to understand and explain correlations. 2 percent noted that the standard of learning in the school was too low. In this context the short training of the teachers and the inability of Standard 5 pupils to speak English was mentioned. According to the majority of the interview partners, the formal system of education also promoted logical thinking, whereby Citumbuka and Ciyawo pupils who were continuously taught in their mother tongue were said to think faster than their age mates who were instructed in Chichewa according to the conventional curriculum.

Ministry of Education staff members
12 staff members of the Ministry of Education were interviewed. Amongst these were 8 Primary Education Advisors, 2 District Education Managers and 2 Ministry members of the Education Methods Advisory Section (EMAS), who are responsible for the development and implementation of new educational methods. 7 of the interviewees were women and 5 were men, wherein the gender distribution in the higher positions was relatively balanced.

Instruction in the mother tongue and psychological development
All of the interview partners welcomed the idea of instruction in the mother tongue because the communication in a familiar language offered the pupils a sense of continuity in the school enrolment, their new phase in life. This would encourage an active participation during the classes. Through the use of the mother tongue, the pupils would be in a better position to follow the lessons, to understand the subject matter and to integrate it into existing mental structures. 75 percent explained that abilities to think and express one's views would be promoted. Through the additional introduction of modern teaching methods, the active participation in forming the lessons would be encouraged; abilities to discuss and to solve problems would be practiced. Through exploratory learning, learner-centred instruction would help to build on existing knowledge through experience. Generally, they had observed that the lessons were more active and

enthusiastic when the children were taught in a familiar language. 84 percent of the interviewed ministry staff members also indicated that the children gained a better understanding of the material and the set tasks if instructed in the mother tongue. The interview partners maintained that instruction in the mother tongue could be implemented in Malawian primary schools, yet they also mentioned a number of hurdles along the way.

Problems in the systematic introduction of mother tongue instruction
For some languages, it is apparently difficult to find a sufficiently high number of teachers who would be willing to live in the villages on a permanent basis. Moreover, the lack of standardised orthography in most Malawian languages and the costs of developing standardised teaching materials were mentioned as a challenge. Two of the interview partners also mentioned the possibility of political tension and national division as problematic factors.

Summary of the interviews
The interviews reflected the test results to a certain extent. With one exception, the interview partners believe that instruction in the mother tongue leads to better and less inhibited communication in class. During discussions, the pupils consciously or unconsciously conversed in the language they were familiar with. Through the use of a language which the pupils know well, they can concentrate on the lessons and can integrate the new knowledge into existing mental structures. Through the use of a familiar language, the pupils are given a sense of continuity while entering this new phase in life, the school enrolment. This would in turn give the pupils the chance to actively participate in class and would minimise possible mental barriers which can occur in a Standard 1 pupil. The representatives of the village communities also saw these problems, yet they placed the main emphasis on the observation that instruction in their own language made the children proud speakers, discouraged prejudices against one's own culture and therefore lead to the maintenance of the culture.

The use of modern teaching methods made the lessons more active and motivated the pupils to actively participate in the lessons, to exercise discussions and enhance problem solving abilities. Recently learnt material solidifies itself through the active exchange of ideas and explaining the material to one's peers. The teacher consciously places the focus on the learners and actively involves them in the lesson design in order to promote critical, problem oriented thinking as well as a creative way of handling materials. Through experiments, the pupils learn to explore properties and reactions of elements and are encouraged to solve problems by themselves. Village representatives appreciate learner-centred methods, as the children could understand concepts and could explain these to family members. In this way the community could indirectly benefit from the classes.

The interview partners however, also voiced criticism, especially with regards to the implementation. The ministry staff members for instance, feared that the country lacked a sufficient number of trained teachers in the respective local languages and that the country wide expansion of instruction in the mother tongue could lead to political tension.

3.7. Summary of Chapter Three

In this chapter, the methodological approach was presented and the instruments used in the study were described. The obtained data was collected with the aid of a picture based intelligence test and interviews with various stakeholders in the Malawian education system. The tests demonstrated that:

1. the use of a familiar language improves and expands the pupil's mental abilities
2. the pilot pupils partly attained better results than the Chichewa speaking pupils.
3. the results between the pilot and control groups of the non-Chichewa speakers clearly deviated, partly significantly.
4. the pupils could be promoted better in their development through instruction in the mother tongue and visible differences between them could be avoided.

In the interviews, it was remarkably noted that:

1. the self-esteem of the pupils and the community is strengthened through the use of local languages in school.
2. prejudices towards one's own culture are reduced and the cultural heritage is maintained.
3. nearly all interview partners hoped for instruction in the mother tongue in order to enable an improved and more open communication in class, to ensure an active participation in the lessons.

4. Results and conclusions

In the last chapter of this study, all the results are summarised and both the theoretical and empirical insights are discussed. Furthermore, the limits of the study and the need for further studies are considered. The study ends on a note about the transferral of multilingual school models into the Malawian language setting and the resulting implications for implementation.

4.1. The relationship between the mother tongue and logical thinking

The presented study is built on the basis of four study questions. Examined was the use of a language which is familiar to the pupil in the early primary school years which may or may not influence the development of selected cognitive operations. To examine this, tests and interviews were conducted in three regions in Malawi (Mangochi, Rumphi and Ntcheu). Approximately two thirds of the children who participated in the study do not speak the national language, Chichewa, in their home environment, but Ciyawo or Citumbuka. From 2004 to the end of 2006, the pupils participated in the "Literacy across the curriculum" pilot project and were divided into pilot and control classes. The difference between the pilot and control classes lay in the language of instruction and the teaching methods. The pilot classes were instructed in their mother tongue during the first three years of primary school and learnt how to read and write in this language. The teachers also used a learner-centred teaching approach and developed their own additional teaching material for the lessons. In the control classes the language of instruction remained Chichewa for all the three language areas and the lessons were generally teacher-centred. In total, 250 pupils participated in this study. The results were used to make conclusions about their ability of deductive thinking. Furthermore, interviews were conducted with parents, teachers, teacher trainers and ministry staff members in the three language areas.

The study examined the hypothesis, whether the pupils who were instructed in a familiar language in their first years of primary school, demonstrated more structured logical thinking than the pupils who were mainly taught in an unfamiliar language.

In the first chapter, a model was developed to illustrate the hypothesis, which was then adapted to the test results. The ordinate axis presented the BIVA test results, the abscissa distinguished between Chichewa mother tongue speakers and non-Chichewa mother tongue speakers. The latter are Citumbuka and Ciyawo speakers.

The pupils' test marks were interpreted with the results that instructing a child in a familiar language, markedly reduces the disadvantage of the pupils with a mother tongue which is not Chichewa (Chilora 2007:13). They performed nearly as well as their Chichewa speaking age mates in the intelligence test, while the control groups – taught in the conventional manner – attained lower test results. The test results of the Chichewa mother tongue speakers were better than the non-Chichewa mother tongue speakers, whereby the pilot group of the non-Chichewa mother tongue speakers nearly achieved the same results as the Chichewa mother tongue speakers. With one exception, the pupils of the pilot group, that is the pupils who were instructed in their mother tongue during their first three years of primary school, solved the set tasks better than the control group.

On average, the control group of the Chichewa speakers attained better marks than the pilot pupils of this language group. The difference between the two groups was in the teaching method, as all pupils were instructed in their mother tongue, Chichewa. The fact that the test results of the control pupils within this language group were partly better than the pilot group indicates that the language of instruction and not the teaching method was the decisive factor. The pilot group of the Citumbuka and Ciyawo speaking groups performed much better than the control groups in these areas. The control groups were taught in Chichewa, using the conventional teaching method.

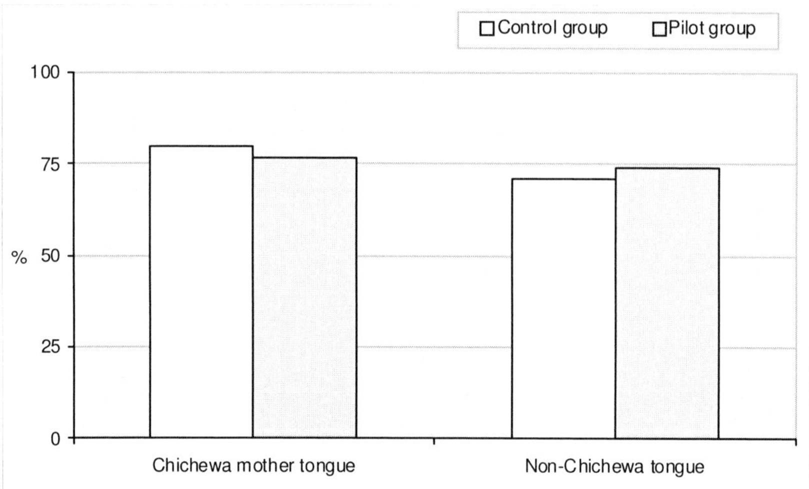

Figure 4.1. Test results presented graphically (Langer 2010:106)

The results of the test confirmed the hypothesis, that the choice of the language of instruction has an obvious influence on the development of logical thinking in the early primary school years. This finding reflects the results of several international studies; even though very few of these researches were conducted in an African context (e.g. Plüddemann 2005:203).

The research findings also concentrated on the study interest of comparing the development of cognitive abilities between classes taught in a familiar language and those instructed in a language that was unfamiliar prior to school enrolment. Here the promotion of deductive thinking in the different learning environments was of interest. The study showed that instructing children in a familiar language promotes the self-esteem and encourages them to actively participate and articulate their thoughts. Concept patterns which have developed in the first language are expanded and stabilised. The learning goes from the familiar to the unfamiliar, as the pupils are acquainted with the medium of instruction and their attention can be focussed on the new concepts and new knowledge. The learning process is not disturbed by communication difficulties. Through the instruction in the familiar language, the pupils learn to read and write in this language. The abilities to speak and hear are already developed and act as supporting agents when learning to read and write in the first language (Peltzer-Karpf and Zangl 1998:8 ff.). The pupils of the pilot group, who were exclusively taught in their mother tongue during the first three years of school, developed the ability of deductive thinking to the same level as their counterparts from the Chichewa speaking group. The interviewed teachers confirmed that the lessons were very multifaceted, as the pupils were interested and participated enthusiastically.

Further areas of focus were the opinions of different stakeholders in the instruction in the mother tongue and its effects on the psychological development. Interviews with various groups, amongst them 39 village inhabitants, 20 parents, 20 teachers, 10 teacher trainers and 12 ministry staff members, served as the data basis. The interviews found that with the exception of one teacher, the interview partners were all in favour of instruction in the mother tongue. Instruction in the mother tongue apparently leads to an improved and more open communication during class. Through the use of a familiar language, the new life situation, the school enrolment, presents continuity. Through active participation in the lessons, mental blockades which can occur in Standard 1 pupils, disappear. The active exchange of ideas in a familiar language and explaining the learnt material to other pupils and to their parents helps to solidify the material. If lessons are conducted in a language, of which the pupils have a good command, the pupils can fully concentrate on the lesson subject and can integrate the new knowledge into pre-existing mental structures. The deficits of other indigenous language speakers were alleviated through instruction in the mother tongue with the appropriate teaching material. This conclusion was confirmed through the test results, in which the pilot group of Citumbuka and Ciyawo speakers nearly obtained the same marks as the Chichewa speakers.

Yet the interview partners also voiced criticism, especially on the question about the practicability of country wide instruction in the mother tongue. Ministry staff for instance commented on the insufficient number of trained teachers in the respective language areas and that this aspect would have to be kept in mind during the recruitment of teaching pupils. They fear that a countrywide expansion of instruction in the mother tongue would lead to political tension.

The empirical study showed a relationship between the language of instruction and deductive thinking abilities in tested pupils. Through the use of the first language, learning and understanding processes are promoted. The existing disadvantage of large parts of the population on grounds of their linguistic background was reduced. The pilot group achieved better results than the control group and nearly caught up with the Chichewa speakers.

In this study, the teaching approach had no significant influence on the ability to demonstrate deductive thinking. On the contrary, the language of instruction was the decisive factor. This can be confirmed through the results of the Chichewa speaking group where the control pupils attained better results, while in all other language groups, the pilot pupils had the better results.

The pupils actively participated in the lessons conducted in the mother tongue, as the instruction in a familiar language strengthened the pupils' self-esteem and the ability to articulate themselves. The results of the LAC study moreover showed that reading, writing and mathematical skills can easily be acquired through the instruction in a familiar language. The LAC project also confirmed that the transferral of the abilities into a new language is eased (compare 2.5.1.).

4.2. Limits of the research and need for further studies

The study obtained its data with the help of a statistical investigation. This always bears the risk of distortion. The empirical research laid its emphasis on establishing a possible influence on the medium of instruction in early primary school years on the development of selected elementary cognitive operations. Although there were visible differences between pilot and control pupils in their approach to the tasks, they were not always statistically significant. This can be explained in respect to at least two factors. Firstly, the test participants were relatively few in number. There were 50 Standard 3 pupils from the Ciyawo speaking area, 25 respectively from the pilot and control classes and in the Citumbuka and Chichewa speaking regions, 200 pupils, respectively 100 pilot and control pupils. On the other hand, the interviews with teachers of the control classes showed that the alternative teaching methods and languages were not used consistently. Teachers in the control classes had to resort to using the pupils' mother tongue, in order to make set tasks understandable. Yet, as shown in the third part of this study, there were visible differences in problem solving techniques. Thirdly, one should not forget that the teachers of the pilot classes conducted lessons in their mother tongue for the first time, so that educational mastery could not be expected.

The use of research assistants or translators presents a further risk, as interpretation can for instance, lead to distortion. The risk was minimised through an intensive orientation in the test and interview induction.

The study tested deductive thinking in two groups of children. The first group learnt in a familiar language, usually its first language. The second group, however, studied in a foreign, but African language at school enrolment. What would be the result if other languages, for instance Ciyawo and English were used instead of the linguistically related Bantu languages Ciyawo and Chichewa or Citumbuka and Chichewa? Would the problem solving differences between the control and pilot pupils be even larger and possibly significant throughout the spectrum? A study, examining the long term effects of instruction in the mother tongue would furthermore be very interesting. In this study, the pupils were tested after a three year period of instruction in a familiar language. What would the results look like after six years of being taught in a multilingual additive system of education? What is the effect of multilingual school education on socioeconomic factors such as the choice of employment and social advancement?

4.3. Possibilities of projecting multilingual education models and new teaching methods on Malawi – putting theory into practice

Chapter Two analysed multilingual education systems and their possible effects. Two models, with a very similar main objective are presented below.

In 2000, Carole Bloch published a study in which she examines the linguistic situation in Malawi and presents ideas of possible education models.[47] She developed three models, which all use the mother tongue as the medium of instruction (Bloch 2000:32 ff.). In the first model (A) the pupils are taught in the mother tongue in one class. Besides the mother tongue, they also learn two languages (English and Chichewa), either simultaneously from Standard 1 (Type A1) or subsequently (English from Standard 1; Chichewa from Standard 4 or 5 – Type A2). In model B, the teacher sporadically switches to English in Standard 3, and English gradually replaces the mother tongue as the medium of instruction (fully from Standard 5). In model C1, Chichewa is taught as a language subject from Standard 1. In contrast to this, Chichewa is taught as a subject from Standard 4 in model C2. Simultaneously a gradual change from the mother tongue as the medium of instruction to English occurs from Standard 3 to 6. Bloch's model C therefore has a mixed language situation in the classroom (e.g. Chichewa + Ciyawo or Chichewa + Citumbuka). In model C1, the pupils study some subjects in their mother tongue. During the school day, the pupils are taught in mixed classes. The children are taught in the respective other mother tongue as their language of instruction until Standard 5, after which the mother tongue is also only taught as a language subject. This model allows a gentle transition to English as the medium of instruction. In C2, the teacher has a good command of both languages.

---

[47] Tabular presentation of the models in Appendix 11.

In 2003, the Malawian Ministry of Education, Science and Technology put forward a model for multilingual education (MoEST 2003a:33f.)[48].This will be presented below and notes about its feasibility are given in the light of the study results. The model is divided into the dominant languages and provides different opportunities for Chichewa dominated regions and non-Chichewa dominated regions of Malawi. Both cases represent a trilingual system, meaning that besides the official languages, Chichewa and English, the pupils learn how to read and speak another local language. Such a system minimises the possible discrimination or disadvantage of large segments of the population (Bamgbose 2000: 16) and takes the existing use of language into account when developing the curriculum (Obura 1990: 176). According to this model, all primary school pupils start off in a familiar language, Citumbuka in the north or Ciyawo along the lakeshore and in the region south of Lake Malawi. Additionally, children who have a different mother tongue (for instance in the towns), receive special support. They receive remedial lessons in order to learn the language of instruction faster and consequently be able to follow the lessons. In the Chichewa speaking regions, the pupils additionally learn one other local language besides Chichewa and English. In the non-Chichewa dominated areas, the children learn Chichewa and English in addition to their first language. The model hopes to create a multilingual alphabetised environment (MoEST 2003a:44). However, the lessons are only instructed in the pupils' first language in the first two years of school and are then conducted in Chichewa. In order to reach a balanced multilingualism, the language must be used for a minimum of six years in school (ADEA 2006:7). The learning of other languages is made easier through conscious reflection on one's own language (Tulasiewicz 2000: 10; Peltzer-Karpf & Zangl 1998:10 f; Barradas 1996:113; List 1995:35; Krashen 1989:69).

With some modifications, both models can enrich the Malawian education system. Through an extension of the proposed two years, in which the mother tongue serves as the medium of instruction, the pupil would reach a high level of verbal and written command of this language. As the level which a speaker can attain in the second language depends on the command of the first language (Skutnabb-Kangas 1981:223; Baker 1988:177; Cenoz Genesee 1998:28), a longer exposure to the first language would lead to a better understanding of other languages. Besides the use of the familiar language as the medium of instruction, the language should also be considered in terms of a subject to be taught (Wolff 2002b:147).

With increased command of and through the use of local languages in public areas, the speakers' pride of their own language and culture, as well as respect for other languages and their speakers would grow (Chimombo 1999:93). Trilingual instruction demands the same efforts from all pupils, regardless of whether they come from a minority or majority language group.

[48] Tabular presentation of the models in Appendix 12.

Such a language policy influences different "areas". The teacher training programme, IPTE, already tries to consider the linguistic background of the teacher students during recruitment.

The interviews in this study found that the teachers were in a dilemma, as the official language policy from 1996 encouraged them to teach the children in their first language during their first four years of primary school. Yet on the ground, the schools lacked appropriate teaching materials and the respective teaching terminology in the local languages. As a result, teachers translated the teaching materials during the lessons and used their own word creations, in order to make the material comprehensible for the pupils. Translating could take up to 50% of their lesson time. The teachers should be equipped with materials and standardised vocabulary in the local languages. Malawi has very enthusiastic linguists and mother tongue speakers of the different indigenous languages, who work as primary school teachers, at the University of Malawi and at the MIE. They have expressed their interest to develop the terminology and the pupil-friendly teaching materials.

The interview partners of this study, nearly unanimously expressed their affirmation for the use of a familiar language in the first primary school years. Since 1999, during annual national language symposia, intellectuals from diverse public services exchange their ideas on the role of Malawi's indigenous languages. Government representatives, who subsequently take the ideas and proposals into the ministry, are also present during these discussions. The accentuation of the linguistic diversity is no doubt a sensitive matter, yet most of the interview partners rated it very positively. Only two interviewees believed that it could lead to political tension and ethnic conflicts.

Learning results can be improved through motivation by creating a literary-rich-environment in the academic and familial surroundings.

This study hopes to present a valid contribution to the current discussion on the education language policy in Malawi. The presented conclusions about a possible influence of a familiar language of instruction in the first primary school years on the development of elementary cognitive operations support the opinions of several cited linguists and pedagogues from Malawi and other countries. These academics demand the right to education in a familiar language for every child and the realisation of multilingual education in Malawi. The education language policy and the question which language future generations of Malawian primary school pupils should learn in, has been a centre of discussion in Malawi since 1999. It remains a hope that the long period of discussion will finally make way for a time of action. Because:

The bird, that does not fly,
Does not know, where the ripe fruits lie.
(From Burundi)

5. Bibliography

Abendroth-Timmer, Dagmar; Breidbach, Stephan (Publ.). 2000. Handlungsorientierung und Mehrsprachigkeit. Frankfurt/Main: Peter Lang.

Accra Declaration. 1996. For the promotion and use of African languages in education. (Online-Source:www.bisharat.net/Documents/Accra96Charter.htm)

ADEA. 2003. The challenge of learning: Improving the quality of basic education in Sub-Saharan Africa. Working document. Association for the Development of Education in Africa (ADEA).

-. 2006. Optimizing learning and education in Africa – the language factor. Working document. Association for the Development of Education in Africa (ADEA).

Aitchinson, Jean. 2003. Words in the mind: An introduction to the mental lexicon. 3rd ed. Oxford: Blackwell Publishing.

Alidou, Hassana; Brock-Utne, Birgit. 2006. Experience I – Teaching practices – Teaching in a familiar language. In: ADEA. *Optimizing learning and education in Africa – the language factor*. Working document. Association for the Development of Education in Africa (ADEA), 75-90.

American Psychological Association. 1993. Guidelines for providers of psychological services to ethnic, linguistic, and culturally diverse populations. *American Psychologist*, 48, 45-48.

Arnold, Wilhelm; Eysenck, Hans Jürgen; Meili, Richard. 1996. Lexikon der Psychologie. Freiburg: Bechtermünz Verlag.

Baker, Colin. 1988. Key issues in bilingualism and bilingual education. Clevedon: Multilingual Matters.

-. 1992. Attitudes and language. Clevedon: Multilingual Matters.

-. 1993. Foundations of bilingual education and bilingualism. 1st ed. Clevedon: Multilingual Matters.

-. 1995. A parents' and teachers' guide to bilingualism. Clevedon: Multilingual Matters.

-. 2006. Foundations of bilingual education and bilingualism. 4th ed. Clevedon: Multilingual Matters.

Baker, Colin; Prys Jones, Sylvia. 1998. Encyclopedia of bilingualism and bilingual education. Clevedon: Multilingual Matters.

Bamgbose, Ayo. 1983. Education in indigenous languages: The West African model of language education. *The Journal of Negro Education*, 57-64.

-. 1984. Mother-tongue medium and scholastic attainment in Nigeria. *Prospects*, 14, (1), 87-93.

-. 1994. Pride and prejudice in multilingualism and development. In: Fardon, Richard; Furniss, Graham: *African languages, development and the state.* London: Routledge, 33-43.

-. 2000. Language and Exclusion. Hamburg: LIT.

Barradas, Olga. 1996. A study of the oral language proficiency of Portuguese bilingual children in London. In: Cline, Tony; Frederickson, Norah. *Curriculum related assessment, Cummins and bilingual children*. Clevedon: Multilingual Matters, 98-115.

Bausch, Karl-Richard; Christ, Herbert; Krumm, Hans-Jürgen. 1995. Handbuch Fremdsprachenunterricht. 3rd ed. Tübingen: Francke Verlag.

Beard, Ruth M. 1969. An outline of Piaget's developmental psychology for pupils and teachers. London: Routledge & Kegan Paul Ltd.

Beatens Beardsmore, Hugo. 1982. Bilingualism: Basic Principles. Clevedon: Multilingual Matters.

Ben-Zeev, Sandra. 1977. The influence of bilingualism on cognitive strategy and cognitive development. *Child Development*, 48, 1009-1018.

Benson, Carol. 2004. Do we expect too much of bilingual teachers? Bilingual teaching in developing countries. In: Brutt-Griffler, Janina; Varghese, Manka. *Bilingualism and language pedagogy*. Clevedon: Multilingual Matters, 112-129.

Benson, Etienne. 2003. Intelligence across cultures. *Monitor on Psychology*, 34 (2), 56-58.

Bialystok, Ellen. 1991. Metalinguistic dimensions of bilingual language proficiency. In: Bialystok, Ellen (Publ.). *Language processing in bilingual children*. Cambridge: Cambridge University Press, 113-140.

Binet, Alfred. 1927. Die neuen Gedanken über das Schulkind. 2nd ed. Leipzig: Verlag Ernst Wunderlich.

Bisika, John J. 1984. Implication of the ability to conserve mass, weight and volume to the learning of Science in primary school. University of Malawi, M.Ed. thesis.

Bleyhl, Werner. 2001. Die schulische Sprachenwahl – Oder: Ist es gleichgültig, in welcher Sprache man denkt? *Fremdsprachen Frühbeginn*, 2, 5-10.

Bloch, Carole. 2000. A pilot study design for the use of mother tongue (local languages) in early primary schooling in Malawi. University of Cape Town.

Bloom, Lois. 1976. Reading in language development. New York: John Wiley and Sons.

-. 1993. The transition from infancy to language. Cambridge: University Press.

BMZ. 2007. Millenniumsentwicklungsziele. Zahlen und Fakten. Bundesministerium für wirtschaftliche Zusammenarbeit und Entwicklung. (Online-Source: http://www.bmz.de/de/zahlen/ millenniumsentwicklungsziele/ mdg2.html)

Borich, Gary D.; Madden, Susan K. 1977. Evaluating classroom instruction: A sourcebook of instruments. Reading, Massachusetts: Addison-Wesley Publishing Company.

Boring, Edwin Garrigues. 1950. A history of experimental psychology. 2nd ed. New York: Appleton-Century-Crofts Inc.

Bortz, Jürgen. 2005. Statistik für Human- und Sozialwissenschaftler. 6th ed. Heidelberg: Springer Medizin Verlag.

Brearley, Molly; Hitchfield, Elizabeth. 1966. A teacher's guide to reading Piaget. London: Routledge & Kegan Paul Ltd.

Brisk, Maria E.; Harrington, Margaret M. 2000. Literacy and bilingualism. Mahwah, New Jersey: Lawrence Erlbaum Associates, Inc.

Brock-Utne, Birgit; Alidou, Hassana. 2006. Experience II – Active pupils – learning through a language they master. In: ADEA. *Optimizing Learning and Education in Africa – the Language Factor*. Working document. Association for the Development of Education in Africa (ADEA), 101-117.

Brown, H. Douglas. 1987. Principles of language learning and teaching. Englewood Cliffs: Prentice Hall.

Bruner, Jerome S. 1962. The process of education. Cambridge: Harvard University Press.

-. 1966. Towards a theory of instruction. New York: Norton.

-. 1986. Actual minds, possible words. Cambridge: Harvard University Press.

-. 1996. The culture of education. Cambridge: Harvard University Press.

-. 1997. Comment on "Beyond competence". *Cognitive Development*, 12, 341-343.

-. 2002. Wie das Kind sprechen lernt. 2nd ed. Bern: Hans Huber Verlag.

Brutt-Griffler, Janina; Varghese, Manka. 2004. Bilingualism and language pedagogy. Clevedon: Multilingual Matters.

Buggle, Franz. 2001. Die Entwicklungspsychologie Jean Piagets. 4th ed. Stuttgart: Kohlhammer.

Bullock, Alan. 1975. A Language for life: Report of the committee of inquiry appointed by the secretary of state for education and science. HMSO.

Butterworth, George. 1994. Infant intelligence. In: Khalfa, Jean (Publ.). *What is Intelligence?* Cambridge: Cambridge University Press, 49-71.

Camilleri, Antoinette. 1995. Bilingualism in education. Heidelberg: Groos.

Cannell, Charles F.; Kahn, Robert L. 1968. Interviewing. In: Lindzey, Gardner; Aronson, Elliott (Publ.). *The Handbook of social psychology*, Vol.2, Research Methods. New York: Addison-Wesley, 526-595.

Carroll, John B. (Publ.) 1956. Language, thought, and reality. Selected writings of Benjamin Lee Whorf. Cambridge, Massachusetts: M.I.T. Press.

Cattell, Ray. 2004. Children's language. 2nd ed. London: Continuum.

Cenoz, Jasone; Genesee, Fred. 1998. Psycholinguistic perspectives on multilingualism and multilingual education. In: Cenoz, Jasone; Genesee, Fred. *Beyond bilingualism*. Clevedon: Multilingual Matters, 16-32.

CLS. 1999. Sociolinguistic survey of four Malawian languages: With special reference to education. Centre for Language Studies (University of Malawi).

Chesterfield, Ray. 1999. Classroom observation tools. USAID: IEQ.

Chilora, Henri. 2000. Literacy development through a local language in a multilingual setting in Malawi. USAID. IEQ Project.

-. 2003. Implementing a multilingual education programme. In: Pfaffe, Joachim Friedrich (Publ). 2003. Implementing Multilingual Education. Proceedings of the Fourth National Symposium on Language Policy and Language Policy Implementation. Lilongwe and Zomba: GTZ and University of Malawi, Centre for Language Studies, 66-76.

-. 2007. Development of literacy in Malawi by using learner's language of play. Domasi: Malawi Institute of Education.

Chilora, Henri; Harris, Abigail. 2000. Teacher's home language versus mother tongue instruction policy. American Institute for Research.

-. 2001. Investigating the role of teacher's home language in mother tongue policy implementation: Evidence from IEQ research findings in Malawi. American Institute for Research.

Chilora, Henri; Jessee, Cassandra L.; Heyman, Cory. 2003. Investigating pupil's performance on mathematics word problems in lower primary school in Malawi. American Institute for Research.

Chilora, Henri; Zembeni, Gibson. 2005. MBTL. Internal evaluation report. MIE, Domasi.

Chimombo, Joseph; Kunje, Demis; Chimuzu, Thokozire; Mchikoma, Clive. 2005a. The SACMEQ II project in Malawi: A study of the conditions of schooling and the quality of education. SACMEQ II Report.

Chimombo, Joseph; Mwale, Livness; Ndalama, Lexon. 2005b. An assessment of schooling conditions and standard one-achievement levels in pre-literacy, pre-numeracy, basic literacy and numeracy in Malawian primary schools. PCAR Baseline Study of 12 Districts. Zomba: Centre for Educational Research & Training, University of Malawi.

Chimombo, Moira. 1999. The multilingual classroom: Fact, fantasy and the future. In: Kamwendo, Gregory H.; Mtenje, Alfred D.; Pfaffe, Joachim, Friedrich; Sandhaas, Bernd (Publ.). *Towards a national language policy in education*. Proceedings of a National Symposium on Language Policy Formulation, Lilongwe and Zomba: GTZ and University of Malawi, Centre for Language Studies, 83-100.

Chomsky, Noam. 1972. Language and mind. San Diego: Harcourt Brace Jovanovich Publ.

-. 1986. Knowledge of language. New York: Praeger.

Cline, Tony; Frederickson, Norah. 1996. Curriculum related assessment, Cummins and bilingual children. Clevedon: Multilingual Matters,

Cohen, Louis; Manion, Lawrence. 1994. Research methods in education. London: Routledge.

Collison, G. Omani. 1974. Concept formation in a second language: A Study of Ghanaian school children. *Harvard Educational Review*, 44 (3), 441-457.

Coombs, Philip H.; Ahmed, Manzoor. 1974. Attacking rural poverty. How nonformal education can help. London: John Hopkins University Press.

-. 1985. The World Crisis in Education. The View from the Eighties. Oxford: Clarenton Press.

Cummins, Jim. 1981. The role of primary language development in promoting educational success for language minority children. In: California State Department of Education (Publ). *Schooling and language minority pupils: A theoretical framework*. Los Angeles: Evaluation, Dissemination and Assessment Center, 3-49.

-. 1984. Bilingualism and special education: Issues in assessment and pedagogy. Austin, Texas: pro ed.

-. 2000. Language, power and pedagogy. Clevedon: Multilingual Matters.

Cummins, Jim; Swain, Merrill. 1986. Bilingualism and education: Aspects of theory, research and practice. London, New York: Longman.

DAPP Malawi. 2006. DAPP Chilangoma Teacher Training College Blantyre. Year Report 2006.

de Lauwe, Paul-Henry Chombard. 1981. The sharing of knowledge and innovative cultures. In: *Domination or sharing? Endogenous development and the transfer of knowledge*. Paris: Unesco Press, 263-288.

Dennett, Daniel. 1994. Language and intelligence. In: Khalfa, Jean (Publ.). *What is Intelligence?* Cambridge: University Press, 161-178.

Diaz, R.M. 1983. Thought and two languages: The impact of bilingualism on cognitive development. *Review of Research in Education*, 10; 23-54.

DTED Malawi. 2013. Open and distance learning intake in TTCs 2010-2012.

Dunkin, Michael J.; Biddle, Bruce J. 1974. The study of teaching. New York: Rinehart & Winston.

Ehindero, Olusola J. 1980. The influence of two languages of instruction on pupils' levels of cognitive development and achievement in science. *Journal for Research in Science Teaching* 17, 4, 283-288.

Elugbe, Ben. 1996. The use of African languages in basic education in Nigeria with particular reference to lower primary and functional literacy. In: Legére, Karsten (Publ). *African languages in basic education – Proceedings of the first workshop on African languages in basic education*. Windhoek: Gamsberg Macmillan Publishers, 23-40.

Evans, Judith L. 1970. Children in Africa: A review of psychological research. New York: Teachers College, University of Columbia.

Fabbro, Franco. 1999. The neurolinguistics of bilingualism. An Introduction. East Sussex: Psychology Press.

Fardon, Richard; Furniss, Graham: African languages, development and the state. London: Routledge.

Field, Andy. 2000. Discovering statistics using SPSS for Windows. London: Sage.

Fishman, Joshua. 2005. A sociology of bilingualism: From home to school and back again. In: Rodriguez-Yánez, Xoán Paulo; Lorenzo Inárez, Anxo M; Ramallo, Fernando (Publ). 2005. *Bilingualism and education: From the family to the school.* München: Lincom.

Flavell, John H. 1963. The developmental psychology of Jean Piaget. Princeton, New Jersey: D. van Nostrand Company.

Fröhlich, Romy; Wutz, Gertraud; Rossmann, Raphael. 2005. Einführung in die sozialwissenschaftliche Datenanalyse. Wiesbaden: Verlag für Sozialwissenschaften.

Fthenakis, Wassilios E.; Sonner, Adelheid; Thrul, Rosemarie; Walbiner, Waltraud. 1985. Bilingual-bikulturelle Entwicklung des Kindes. München: Hueber.

Genesee, Fred. 1987. Learning through two languages. Cambridge: Newbury House Publishers.

Goody, Esther. 1995. Social intelligence and interaction. Cambridge: University Press.

Gordon, Raymond G., Jr. (Publ). 2005. Ethnologue: Languages of the World. 15th ed. Dallas: SIL International. (Online: http://www.ethnologue.com/show_country.asp?name=MW)

Goswami, Usha. 2001. So denken Kinder. Bern: Huber Verlag.

Government of Malawi. 2006. Malawi Growth and Development Strategy 2006-2011.

Grigorenko, Elena L. 1998. Mastering tools of the mind in schools (Trying out Vygotsky's ideas in classrooms). In: Sternberg, Robert J.; Williams, Wendy M. (Publ.) *Intelligence, instruction and assessment.* Mahwah, New Jersey: Lawrence Erlbaum, 201-231.

Grosjean, Francois. 1982. Life with two languages. Cambridge: Harvard University Press.

Grundy, Peter. 2000. The role of language in language learning: A focus on relevant theories. In: Abendroth-Timmer, Dagmar; Breidbach, Stephan (Publ). *Handlungsorientierung und Mehrsprachigkeit.* Frankfurt/Main: Peter Lang, 97-106.

Guthke, Jürgen. 1978. Ist Intelligenz meßbar? Berlin: Deutscher Verlag der Wissenschaften.

-. 1996. Intelligenz im Test. Göttingen; Zürich: Vandenhoeck und Ruprecht.

Gwazanga, B.S.[49] 1988. Project in primary education promotion of effective teaching and learning in primary schools. Malawi Institute of Education.

Hakuta, Kenji. 1986. Mirror of language. New York: Basic Books.

-. 1985. Cognitive development in bilingual instruction. *Issues in English Development*, 63-67.

[49] Found at the library of Malawi Institute of Education (MIE), Domasi.

-. 1990. Language and cognition in bilingual children. In: Padilla, Amado M.; Fairchild, Halford H.; Valadez, Concepción M. (Publ.). *Bilingual Education.* Newbury Park, London: SAGE, 47-59.

Hakuta, Kenji; Ferdman, Bernardo M.; Diaz, Rafael M. 1987. Bilingualism and cognitive development: Three perspectives. In: Rosenberg, Sheldon E. (Publ.) *Advances in applied psycholinguistics. Vol II: Reading, writing and language learning.* Cambridge: Cambridge University Press, 284-319.

Heine, Bernd; Schadeberg, Thilo C.; Wolff, Ekkehard H. (Publ.) 1981. Die Sprachen Afrikas. Hamburg: Buske.

Heine, Bernd; Nurse, Derek. (Publ.). 2000. African Languages. An Introduction. Cambridge: Cambridge University Press.

Helfferich, Cornelia. 2005. Die Qualität qualitativer Daten. 2nd ed. Wiesbaden: Verlag für Sozialwissenschaften.

Heugh, Kathleen. 2006. Theory and practice – Language education models in Africa: research, design, decision-making, and outcomes. In: ADEA. *Optimizing Learning and Education in Africa – the Language Factor.* Working document. Association for the Development of Education in Africa (ADEA), 56-84.

Hildebrand, Karl-Heinrich. 1991. ‚Bookish' knowledge or empowering capacities? Frankfurt/Main: Verlag für Interkulturelle Kommunikation.

Hoffmann, Charlotte. 1991. An introduction to bilingualism. London, New York: Longman.

Ianco-Worrall, Anita D. 1972. Bilingualism and cognitive development. *Child Development*, 43, 1390-1400.

IMF. 2002. Malawi Poverty Reduction Strategy Paper. International Monetary Fund.

Ingram, David. 1989. First language acquisition. Cambridge: Cambridge University Press.

Inhelder, Bärbel; Piaget, Jean. 1958. The growth of logical thinking from childhood to adolescence. London: Routledge & Kegan Paul Ltd.

Jahoda, Gustav. 1956. Assessment of abstract behaviour in a Non-Western culture. *Journal of Abnormal and Social Psychology*, 53, 237-243.

Jarvis, Lorna H.; Danks, Joseph H.; Merriman, William E. 1995. The effect of bilingualism on cognitive ability: A test of the level of bilingualism hypothesis. *Applied Psycholinguistics*, 16, 293-308.

Kachaso, Leonard. 1988. Language effects on pupils performance in Mathematics word problems in Standard seven. University of Malawi, M. Ed. thesis.

Kadzamira, Esme; Rose, Pauline. 2003. Can free primary education meet the needs of the poor?: Evidence from Malawi. *International Journal of Educational Development*, 23, 501-516.

Kamwendo, Gregory H.; Mtenje, Alfred D.; Pfaffe, Joachim, Friedrich; Sandhaas, Bernd (Publ.). 1999. *Towards a national language policy in education.* Proceedings of a National Symposium on Language Policy Formulation, Lilongwe and Zomba: GTZ and University of Malawi, Centre for Language Studies.

Kamwendo, Gregory H. 1997. Language policy in Malawi. *Zimbabwe Journal of Educational Research*, 9 (2), 203-215.

-. 2001. Chichewa or Chinyanja? Problems in the naming of a cross-border language. Paper presented at LASU Conference, August 2001. University of Botswana.

-. 2004. Language policy in health services: A sociolinguistic study of a Malawian referral hospital. Helsinki: University Press.

Karmiloff-Smith, Annette. 1992. Beyond modularity. A developmental perspective on cognitive science. Cambridge, Massachusetts: M.I.T. Press.

Kayambazinthu, Edrinnie. 1998. The language planning situation in Malawi. *Journal of Multilingual and Multicultural Development*, Vol. 19 (5+6), 369-439.

Kelly, Michael. 1974. Products and Processes in cognitive development: Some comparative data on the performance of school-age children in different cultures. *British Journal of Educational Psychology*, 44, 248-265.

Kembo, Jane. 2000. Language in education and language learning in Africa. IN: Webb, Vic; Kembo-Sure (Publ). *African voices.* Cape Town: Oxford University Press Southern Africa, 286-311.

Kerlinger, Fred N. 1979. Grundlagen der Sozialwissenschaften. Weinheim: Beltz-Verlag.

KfW. 2004. Projektpapier Primarschulbildung II. Kreditanstalt für Wiederaufbau. Frankfurt. (Online-Source: http://www.kfw-entwicklungsbank.de/DE_Home/Laender_und_Projekte/AfrikaSubs73/Zentralafr18/Malawi80/PKD_extern_17891_Bildung_II_Sep04.pdf)

Khalfa, Jean (Publ.) 1994. What is Intelligence? Cambridge: Cambridge University Press.

Kholowa, Foster; Rose, Pauline. 2007. Parental or policy maker misunderstandings? Contextual dilemmas of pre-schooling for poverty reduction in Malawi. *International Journal of Educational Development*, 27, 458-472.

Ki-Zerbo, Joseph. 1990. Educate or perish: Africa's impasse and progress. Dakar, Abidjan: UNESCO-UNICEF.

Kishindo, Pascal. 1998. Politics of language in contemporary Malawi. In: Phiri, Kings Mbacazwa; Ross, Kenneth R. (Publ.). Democratization in Malawi: A Stocktaking. Blantyre: CLAIM, 252-280.

-. 1999. Implementing language policy decisions in education: Lessons from research. In: Kamwendo, Gregory H.; Mtenje, Alfred D.; Pfaffe, Joachim, Friedrich; Sandhaas, Bernd (Publ.). *Towards a national language policy in education*. Proceedings of a National Symposium on Language Policy Formulation, Lilongwe and Zomba: GTZ and University of Malawi, Centre for Language Studies, 28-40.

-. 2003. Towards a model of mother tongue education for Malawi. In: Pfaffe, Joachim Friedrich (Publ.). *Implementing multilingual education*. Proceedings of the fourth National Symposium on Language Policy and Language Policy Implementation, Lilongwe and Zomba: GTZ and University of Malawi, Centre for Language Studies, 85-92.

-. In press. Proceedings of the 6th National Symposium on Literacy for development: The role of African languages, Lilongwe and Zomba: GTZ and University of Malawi, Centre for Language Studies.

Klauer, Karl Josef. 1973. Das Experiment in der pädagogisch-psychologischen Forschung. Münster: Waxmann.

Klix, Friedhart. 1983. Begabungsforschung – ein neuer Weg in der kognitiven Intelligenz-diagnostik. *Zeitschrift für Psychologie*, 191, 360-387.

-. 1993. Erwachendes Denken. Heidelberg: Spektrum Akademischer Verlag.

Kloss, Heinz. 1969. Research possibilities on group bilingualism. A report. Quebec: International Center for Research on Bilingualism.

Kodjo, Samuel. 1973. Probleme der Akkulturation in Afrika. Meisenheim am Glan: Anton Hain.

Konrad, Klaus. 2005. Mündliche und schriftliche Befragung. Ein Lehrbuch, 3rd ed., Forschung, Statistik & Methoden, Vol. 4. Landau: Verlag Empirische Pädagogik.

Kranz, Helger T. 1997. Einführung in die klassische Testtheorie. 4th ed. Eschborn: Verlag Dietmar Klotz.

Krashen, Stephen. 1985. The input hypothesis: Issues and implications. London: Longman.

-. 1987. Principles and practice in second language acquisition. New York: Prentice-Hall International.

-. 1988. Second language acquisition and second language learning. New York: Prentice-Hall International.

-. 1989. Language acquisition and language education. New York: Prentice-Hall International.

-. 1997. Why Bilingual Education? *Review of Educational Research*, 55, 269-316.

Kuckartz, Udo. 2005. Einführung in die computergestützte Analyse qualitativer Daten. Wiesbaden: Verlag für Sozialwissenschaften.

Kunje, Demis. 2002. The Malawi integrated in-service teacher education programme: An experiment with mixed-mode training. *International Journal of Educational Development*, 22, 305-320.

Lamberti, Georg. 2006. Zur Entwicklung der Psychometrie nach James McKeen Cattell (1860-1944). In: Lamberti, Georg (Publ.) *Intelligenz auf dem Prüfstand – 100 Jahre Psychometrie*. Göttingen: Vandenhoeck & Ruprecht, 9-21.

Langer, Anja. 2010. Unterrichtssprache und kognitive Entwicklung. Fallstudien aus Malawi. Berlin: LIT.

Lee, Patrick. 1996. Cognitive development in bilingual children: A case for bilingual instruction in early childhood education. *The Bilingual Research Journal*, Summer/Fall 1996, 20, 3 & 4, 499-522.

Lefrançois, Guy R. 2006. Psychologie des Lernens. 4th ed.; Berlin: Springer.

Legére, Karsten (Publ). 1996. African languages in basic education – Proceedings of the first workshop on African languages in basic education. Okahandja, 18.-23. September 1995. Windhoek: Gamsberg Macmillan Publishers.

Lenneberg, Eric H. 1972. Biologische Grundlagen der Sprache. New York: John Wiley & Sons.

Lienert, Gustav A. 1961. Testaufbau und Testanalyse. 3rd ed. Weinheim: Beltz Verlag.

Light, Paul; Sheldon, Sue; Woodhead, Martin (Hsrg). 1999. Learning to think. London: Routledge

Lightbown, Patsy M.; Spada, Nina. 2006. How languages are learned. 3rd ed. Oxford: University Press.

Lindzey, Gardner; Aronson, Elliott (Publ.) 1968. The Handbook of social psychology, Vol.2, Research Methods. New York: Addison-Wesley.

List, Gudula. 1995. Psycholinguistik und Sprachpsychologie. In: Bausch, Karl-Richard; Christ, Herbert; Krumm, Hans-Jürgen. *Handbuch Fremdsprachenunterricht*. 3rd ed. Tübingen: Francke Verlag, 31-38.

Loizou, Maria; Stuart, Morag. 2003. Phonological awareness in monolingual and bilingual English and Greek five-year-olds. *Journal of Research in Reading*, 26 (1), 3-18.

Lyman, Howard B. 1963. Test, scores and what they mean. Englewood Cliffs, N.J.: Prentice-Hall, Inc.

Macnamara, John. 1967. The effects of instruction in a weaker language. *Journal of social issues*, 23 (2), 121-135.

Matiki, Alfred J. 2006. Literacy, ethnolinguistic diversity and transitional bilingual education in Malawi. *The International Journal of Bilingual Education and Bilingualism*, 9 (2), 239-254.

Matunga, I.J.[50] 1992. A study to investigate causes of absenteeism at Muwale Free Primary School. Malawi Institute of Education.

Mayring, Philipp. 2002. Qualitative Sozialforschung. 5th ed. Weinheim: Beltz Verlag.

[50] Found at the library of Malawi Institute of Education (MIE), Domasi.

Mbano, Nellie Mathembo. 2001. Exploring the use of cognitive acceleration through science education. (CASE) Intervention programme in secondary school classes in Malawi. London: King's College. (Not published PhD thesis)
McLaughlin, Barry. 1984. Second language acquisition in childhood. 2nd ed. Hillsdale, New Jersey: Erlbaum.
-. 1987. Theories of second-language learning. London: Edward Arnold.
Mchazime, Hartford. 2001. Effects of English as Medium as Instruction on pupils' academic achievement in Social Studies in Primary Schools in Malawi. University of South Africa. (Not published PhD thesis).
-. 2003a. Literacy across the curriculum. Report. GTZ-BEP.
-. 2003b. Implementing Multilingual Education in an African Setting. In: Pfaffe, Joachim F. *Implementing Multilingual Education*. Proceedings of the Fourth National Symposium on Language Policy and Language Policy Implementation. Lilongwe and Zomba: GTZ and University of Malawi, Centre for Language Studies, 14-25.
Mertens, Donna M. 1998. Research methods in education and psychology: Integrating diversity with quantitative & qualitative approaches. Thousand Oaks: SAGE.
MIE. 2003. School Selection Report. Malawi Institute of Education.
Milner, Grace; Chimombo, Joseph; Banda, Thokozire; Mchikoma, Clive. 2001. The quality of education: Some policy suggestions based on a survey of schools - Malawi. An interim report. SACMEQ Policy Research Report. Paris: UNESCO.
Mills, Richard W.; Mills, Jean. 1993. Bilingualism in the primary school. London, New York: Routledge.
MoE. 2004. Malawi. Primary School Syllabuses.
MoESC. 1991. Malawi. Primary School Teaching Syllabus. English. St. 1-8. Ministry of Education, Sports and Culture.
-. 2001. Malawi Education Sector: Policy & Investment Framework (PIF).
MoE&VT. 2006a. EMIS Annual Education Statistics 2006. Ministry of Education and Vocational Training. Education Management Information System (EMIS).
-. 2006b. National Education Statistics. Ministry of Education and Vocational Training.
MoEST. 1996. Use of mother tongue as medium of instruction in Standard 1, 2, 3 and 4. A circular from the Secretary for Education, Science and Technology to education institutions. (Ref. No. IN/2/4 dated 28 March, 1996) Ministry of Education, Science and Technology.
-. 2003a. Primary School Language Survey in Malawi: Final Report.
-. 2003b. Malawi Primary Education Curriculum and Assessment Framework. Draft.
MRE. 2007. Education for all: The Malawi language policy in education. Draft. Ministry Responsible for Education.

Mkandawire, Mathiuz Tiwaone S. 2004. Attitudes and views on local languages as media of instruction in Malawi. Blacksburg, Virginia. Unpublished M.Ed. thesis.

Moto, Francis. 1999. Language, education and democracy. In: Kamwendo, Gregory H.; Mtenje, Alfred D.; Pfaffe, Joachim, Friedrich; Sandhaas, Bernd (Publ.). *Towards a national language policy in education*. Proceedings of a National Symposium on Language Policy Formulation, Lilongwe and Zomba: GTZ and University of Malawi, Centre for Language Studies, 53-81.

Mtenje, Alfred. In press. Proceedings of the 6th National Symposium on Literacy for development: The role of African languages, Lilongwe and Zomba: GTZ and University of Malawi, Centre for Language Studies.

Mussen, Paul H. 1963. The psychological development of the child. Englewood Cliffs: Prentice-Hall.

Nambuzi, R.[51] 1991. Effect of motivation on lateness at Chikuli primary school. Malawi Institute of Education.

Nantchito, V.R.[52] 1992. A study to alleviate the problem of absenteeism through a staff supported programme. Malawi Institute of Education.

National Statistical Office (NSO). 2004. Malawi demographic and health survey. Zomba: Malawi National Statistical Office.

Nelde, Peter H. (Publ.) 1990. Plurilingua IX: Language Attitude and Language Conflict. Bonn: Dümmler.

Nyirenda, Shem Mark. 2003. How best can mother tongue education be implemented – The case of Citumbuka in Northern Malawi. In: Pfaffe, Joachim Friedrich (Publ.). *Implementing multilingual education*. Proceedings of the fourth National Symposium on Language Policy and Language Policy Implementation, Lilongwe and Zomba: GTZ and University of Malawi, Centre for Language Studies, 122-127.

Obura, Anna P. 1990. Language in Conflict in Education in Anglophone Africa. In: Nelde, Peter H. (Publ.). *Plurilingua IX: Language Attitude and Language Conflict*. Bonn: Dümmler, 175-193.

Oevermann, Ulrich. 1971. Schichtenspezifische Formen des Sprachverhaltens und ihr Einfluss auf die kognitiven Prozesse. In: Roth, Heinrich. *Begabung und Lernen*. Stuttgart: Klett, 297-356.

Padilla, Amado M.; Fairchild, Halford H.; Valadez, Concepción M. (Publ.). 1990. Bilingual Education. Newbury Park, London: SAGE.

Peal, Elizabeth; Lambert, Wallace E. 1962. The relation of bilingualism to intelligence. *Psychological Monographs*, 76, 1-23.

Peltzer-Karpf, Annemarie; Zangl, Renate. 1998. Die Dynamik des frühen Fremdsprachenerwerbs. Tübingen: Gunter Narr Verlag.

[51] Found at the library of Malawi Institute of Education (MIE), Domasi.

[52] Found at the library of Malawi Institute of Education (MIE), Domasi.

Penfield, Wilder; Roberts, Lamar. 1959. Speech and brain mechanisms. Princeton: Princeton University Press.

Pfaffe, Joachim Friedrich (Publ). 2000. Local languages in education, science and technology. Proceedings of the Second National Symposium on Language Policy Formulation. Lilongwe and Zomba: GTZ and University of Malawi, Centre for Language Studies.

-. 2003. Implementing Multilingual Education. Proceedings of the Fourth National Symposium on Language Policy and Language Policy Implementation. Lilongwe and Zomba: GTZ and University of Malawi, Centre for Language Studies.

Pflaum, Susanna W. 1986. The development of language and literacy in young children. Columbus: Charles E. Merrill Publ.

Philp, Hugh; Kelly, Max. 1992. Cognitive development and language: some comparative cross-cultural data. Tilburg: Tilburg University Press.

Phiri, Kings Mbacazwa; Ross, Kenneth R. (Publ.) 1998. Democratization in Malawi: A Stocktaking. Blantyre: CLAIM

Piaget, Jean. 1951. Play, dreams and imitation in childhood. Melbourne: William Heinemann Ltd.

-. 1959. The language and thought of the child. 3rd ed. London: Routledge & Kegan Paul Ltd.

-. 1967. Six psychological studies. New York: Vintage Books.

-. 1969. Judgment and reasoning in the child. 5th ed. London: Lowe & Brydone Ltd.

-. 1972. Theorien und Methoden der modernen Erziehung. Wien: Molden Verlag.

-. 1991. Die Psychologie des Kindes. 4th ed. München: Deutscher Taschenbuch Verlag.

-. 1992. Psychologie der Intelligenz. 3rd ed. Stuttgart: Klett-Cotta.

-. 1999. Über Pädagogik. Weinheim: Beltz Verlag.

Plüddemann, Peter. 2005. Bilingual schooling in post-apartheid South Africa. In: Rodriguez-Yánez, Xoán Paulo; Lorenzo Inárez, Anxo M; Ramallo, Fernando (Publ). *Bilingualism and education: From the family to the school.* München: Lincom, 201-213.

Pontecorvo, Clotilde; Sterponi, Laura. 2002. Learning to argue and reason through discourse in educational settings. In: Wells, Gordon; Claxton, Gray (Publ). *Learning for life in the 21st century.* Oxford: Blackwell Publishing, 127-140.

Ponterotto, Joseph G.; Casas, J. Manuel; Suzuki, Lisa A.; Alexander, Charlene M. (Publ.). 1995. Handbook of multicultural counselling. Thousand Oaks, CA: Sage.

Pota, Peter P. 2001. Classroom experiences in teaching through Chichewa or English in a predominantly Ciyawo speaking area. In: Pfaffe, Joachim Friedrich (Publ.). *Proceedings of the 3rd National Symposium on Language Policy and Language Policy Implementation.* Lilongwe and Zomba: GTZ and University of Malawi, Centre for Language Studies, 145-150.

Prah, Kwesi Kwaa. 1995. African languages for the mass education of Africans. Bonn: DSE.

Quay, Suzanne. 2001. Managing linguistic boundaries in early trilingual development. In: Cenoz, Jasone; Genesee, Fred (Publ). *Trends in Bilingual Acquisition.* Amsterdam: John Benjamins Publishing, 149-199.

Ramseger, Jörg. 2001. Evaluation des Konzepts des muttersprachlichen Unterrichts im "Projet Education de Base". Eschborn: GTZ.

Richardson, Ken. 1991. Understanding intelligence. Bristol: Open University Press.

Robbins, Dorothy. 2001. Vygotsky's psychology-philosophy: a metaphor for language theory and learning. New York: Kluwer Academic.

Rodriguez-Yánez, Xoán Paulo; Lorenzo Inárez, Anxo M; Ramallo, Fernando (Publ). 2005. Bilingualism and education: From the family to the school. München: Lincom.

Rogge, Klaus-Eckart (Publ.). 1995. Methodenatlas für Sozialwissenschaftler. Berlin: Springer.

Rose, Pauline. 2002. Cost-sharing in Malawian primary schooling: from the Washington to the post-Washington consensus., University of Sussex, (Not published PhD thesis). Cited in: Kadzamira, Esme; Rose, Pauline. 2003. Can free primary education meet the needs of the poor?: Evidence from Malawi. *International Journal of Educational Development*, 23, 501-516.

Rösing, Ina. 2004. Intelligenz und Dummheit. Kröning: Asanger.

-. 2005. Weisheit. Meterware, Maßschneiderei, Missbrauch. Kröning: Asanger.

Roth, Erwin (Publ). 1980. Intelligenz: Aspekte, Probleme, Perspektiven. Stuttgart: Kohlhammer.

Roth, Heinrich. 1990. Begabung und Lernen. Stuttgart: Klett.

Roy-Campell, Zaline M. 2001: Empowerment through language: the African experience in Tanzania and beyond. Trenton, Asmara: Africa World Press.

Saer, D. J. 1923. The effect of bilingualism on intelligence. *The British Journal of Psychology*, 14 (1), 25-38.

Schaarschmidt, Uwe; Ricken, Gabi; Kieschke, Ulf; Preuß, Ulrich. 2004. Bildbasierter Intelligenztest für das Vorschulalter (BIVA). Göttingen, Bern, Toronto, Seattle: Hogrefe-Verlag für Psychologie.

Schank, Roger; Birnbaum, Lawrence. 1994. Enhancing intelligence. In: Khalfa, Jean (Publ.). *What is Intelligence?* Cambridge: University Press, 72-106.

Schmid, Holger. 1992. Psychologische Tests: Theorie und Konstruktion. Freiburg: Universitätsverlag.

Schnell, Rainer; Hill, Paul B.; Esser, Elke. 2005. Methoden der empirischen Sozialforschung. 7th ed. München: R. Oldenbourg.
Schönpflug, Wolfgang; Schönpflug, Ute. 1995. Psychologie. 3rd ed. Weinheim: Beltz Psychologie VerlagsUnion.
Schönpflug, Ute. 1977. Psychologie des Erst- und Zweitspracherwerbs. Stuttgart: Kohlhammer Verlag.
Schubert, Jane G.; Prouty-Harris, Diane. 2003. Accelerating paths to quality: A multi-faceted reality. ADEA 2003 Biennale Papers.
Serpell, Robert. 1984. Research on cognitive development in Sub-Saharan Africa. *International Journal of Behavioral Development*, 7 (2), 111-127.
-. 1993. The significance of schooling: Life journeys in an African society. Cambridge: Cambridge University Press.
Skinner, Burrhus Frederic. 1957. Verbal behaviour. New York: Appleton-Century-Crofts.
Skutnabb-Kangas, Tove. 1981. Bilingualism or Not? The education of minorities. Clevedon: Multilingual Matters.
Slobin, Dan I. 1986. The crosslinguistic study of language acquisition. Hillsdale, N.J.: Lawrence Erlbaum Association.
Sprung, Lothar; Sprung, Helga. 1984. Grundlagen der Methodologie und Methodik der Psychologie. Berlin: Deutscher Verlag der Wissenschaften.
Sternberg, Robert J. (Publ.). 2000. Handbook of intelligence. Cambridge: Cambridge University Press.
Sternberg, Robert J.; Forsythe, George B.; Hedlund, Jennifer; Horvath, Joseph A.; Wagner, Richard K.; Williams, Wendy M.; Snook, Scott A.; Grigorenko, Elena L. 2000. Practical intelligence in everyday life. Cambridge: Cambridge University Press.
Sternberg, Robert J.; Williams, Wendy M. (Publ.) 1998. Intelligence, instruction and assessment. Mahwah, New Jersey: Lawrence Erlbaum.
Stuart, Janet. 2002. College tutors: a fulcrum for change? *International Journal of Educational Development*, 22, 367-379.
Tadadjeu, Maurice. 1997. Report of the Intergovernmental conference on language policies in Africa. Held in Harare, Zimbabwe, 17-21 March 1997. Yaounde: NACALCO.
Terhart, Ewald. 1999. Konstruktivismus und Unterricht. Gibt es einen neuen Ansatz in der Allgemeinen Didaktik? *Zeitschrift für Pädagogik*, 45, 629-647.
Tharp, Roland; Gallimore, Ronald. 1991. A theory of teaching as assisted performance. In: Light, Paul; Sheldon, Sue; Woodhead, Martin (Hsrg). *Learning to think*. London: Routledge, 42-61.
The Nation. *Daily Newspaper*. 21 June 1996; 22 June 1996; 29 April 2005; 6 December 2006; 23 January 2007.
Thomas, Wayne P.; Collier, Virginia. 1997. School effectiveness for language minority pupils. Washington: National Clearinghouse for Bilingual Education.

-. 2001. A national study of school effectiveness for language minority pupils' long-term academic achievement. Final report executive summary (Online-Source: http://www.crede.ucsc.edu/research/ llaa/1.1_ final.html)

Tiede, Elke. 2005. Literacy across the curriculum: A study piloting children's first language and learner-centred teaching methods in Standard One Classes. GTZ-BEP.

Tulasiewicz, Witold. 2000. Whither language awareness? Enhancing the literacy of the language user. In: White, Lana J.; Maylath, Bruce; Adams, Anthony; Couzijn, Michel. *Language awareness*. Amsterdam: Amsterdam University Press, 5-20.

UNESCO. 1951. Meeting of experts on the use of vernacular languages. Paris.

-. 1962. Final report: Meeting of ministers of education of African countries participating in the implementation of the Addis Ababa plan. Paris: UNESCO Publishing.

-. 1990. World declaration on Education for All: Meeting basic learning needs. (Online-Source:www.unesco.org/education/efa/ed_for_all/background/ jomtien_declaration.shtml)

-. 1994. World declaration on Education for All. Framework for Action to meet Basic Learning Needs. 3rd ed. Paris: UNESCO Publishing.

-. 1998. Lernfähigkeit: Unser verborgener Reichtum. UNESCO-Bericht zur Bildung für das 21.Jahrhundert, 2nd ed. Paris: UNESCO Publishing.

-. 2000a. World Education Forum. Dakar Framework for Action.

-. 2000b. Education for All 2000 Assessment Country Report Malawi. (Online: http://unesco.org/education/wef/countryreports/malawi/ rapport_2.html)

-. 2004. The development of education in Malawi. Report for the 47th Session of the International Conference on Education, Geneva, 7th – 11th September 2004.

-. 2005. EFA Global Monitoring Report 2005.

-. 2007. EFA Global Monitoring Report 2007.

UNESCO Institute for Statistics. 2005. Education in Malawi.

UNICEF. 2009. and 2005. Country Statistics – Malawi. (Online: http://www.unicef.org/infobycountry/malawi_statistics.html)

United Nations. 2001. Common Country Assessment of Malawi. Lilongwe.

Vithal, Renuka & Jonathan Jansen. 1997. Designing your first research proposal. A manual for researchers in education and the social sciences. Durban: Juta & Co. Ltd.

von Humboldt, Wilhelm. 1963. Schriften zur Sprachphilosophie. Stuttgart: J.G. Cotta'sche Buchhandlung.

Vygotsky, Lev Semenovich. 1962. Thought and language. (Published and translated by Hanfmann, Eugenia; Vakar, Gertrude) Cambridge, Massachusetts: M.I.T. Press.

-. 1978. Mind in society: The development of higher psychological processes. Cambridge: Harvard University Press.

-. 1986. Thought and language. (Publd. by A. Kozulin) Cambridge: MIT Press.

-. 1998. The collected works of L. S. Vygotsky. 5th ed.; New York: Plenum Press.

-. 2002. Denken und Sprechen. (Publd. and translated by Lompscher, Joachim; Rückriem, Georg) Weinheim: Beltz Verlag.

Wagner, Daniel A. 1993. Literacy, culture and development: Becoming literate in Marocco. Cambridge: Cambridge University Press.

Walker, Rob; Adelman, Clem. 1975. A guide to classroom observation. London: Methuen & Co Ltd.

Watson, Anne; Mason, John. 1998. Questions and prompts for mathematical thinking. Derby: Association of Teachers of Mathematics.

Webb, Vic; Kembo-Sure. 2000. African voices. Cape Town: Oxford University Press Southern Africa.

Weinreich, Uriel. 1953. Languages in contact: Findings and problems. New York: Columbia university.

Wells, Gordon; Claxton, Gray (Publ). 2002. Learning for life in the 21st century. Oxford: Blackwell Publishing.

Weskamp, Ralf. 2003. Fremdsprachenunterricht entwickeln. Hannover: Schroedel Verlag.

White, Lana J.; Maylath, Bruce; Adams, Anthony; Couzijn, Michel. 2000. Language awareness. Amsterdam: Amsterdam University Press

Wolff, Dieter. 2002a. Fremdsprachenlernen als Konstruktion. Frankfurt/Main: Peter Lang.

Wolff, Ekkehard H. 1981. Die Erforschung der afrikanischen Sprachen: Geschichte und Konzeption. In: Heine, Bernd; Schadeberg, Thilo C.; Wolff, Ekkehard H. (Publ.) *Die Sprachen Afrikas*. Hamburg: Buske, 17-43.

-. 2000. Language and Society. In: Heine, Bernd; Nurse, Derek. (Publ.) *African Languages. An Introduction*, Cambridge: Cambridge University Press, 298-347.

-. 2002b. The African Language Question. In: Owino, Francis R. (Publ.) *Speaking African. African languages in education and development*. Cape Town: Centre for Advanced Studies of African Society (CASAS), 129-148.

-. 2004. Marketing multilingual education in Africa. Keynote Address. In: Proceedings of the 3rd International ADALEST Conference – 5th Malawian National Language Symposium, Lilongwe and Zomba: GTZ and University of Malawi, Centre for Language Studies, 117-158.

Wong Fillmore, Lily. 1991. Second-language learning in children: A model of language learning in social context. In: Bialystok, Ellen (Publ.). *Language processing in bilingual children*. Cambridge: Cambridge University Press, 49-69.

Woods, Antony; Fletcher, Paul; Hughes, Arthur. 1986. Statistics in language studies. Cambridge: Cambridge University Press.

Wright, Daniel B. 1997. Understanding statistics: An introduction for the social sciences. London: Sage.

6. Appendix

App. 1: The Malawian Education System
App. 2: Interview Schedule for Community (ISC)
App. 3: Interview Schedule Teachers (IST)
App. 4: Interview Schedule for Teacher Trainers (ISTT)
App. 5: Interview Schedule for Ministry Officials (ISM)
App. 6: Code ISC
App. 7: Code IST
App. 8: Code ISTT
App. 9: Code ISM
App. 10: Tables for Test Evaluation
App. 11: Multilingual Education Models based on Bloch
App. 12: Multilingual Education Models based on MoEST
App. 13: Pictures from the data collection

App. 1: The Malawian Education System

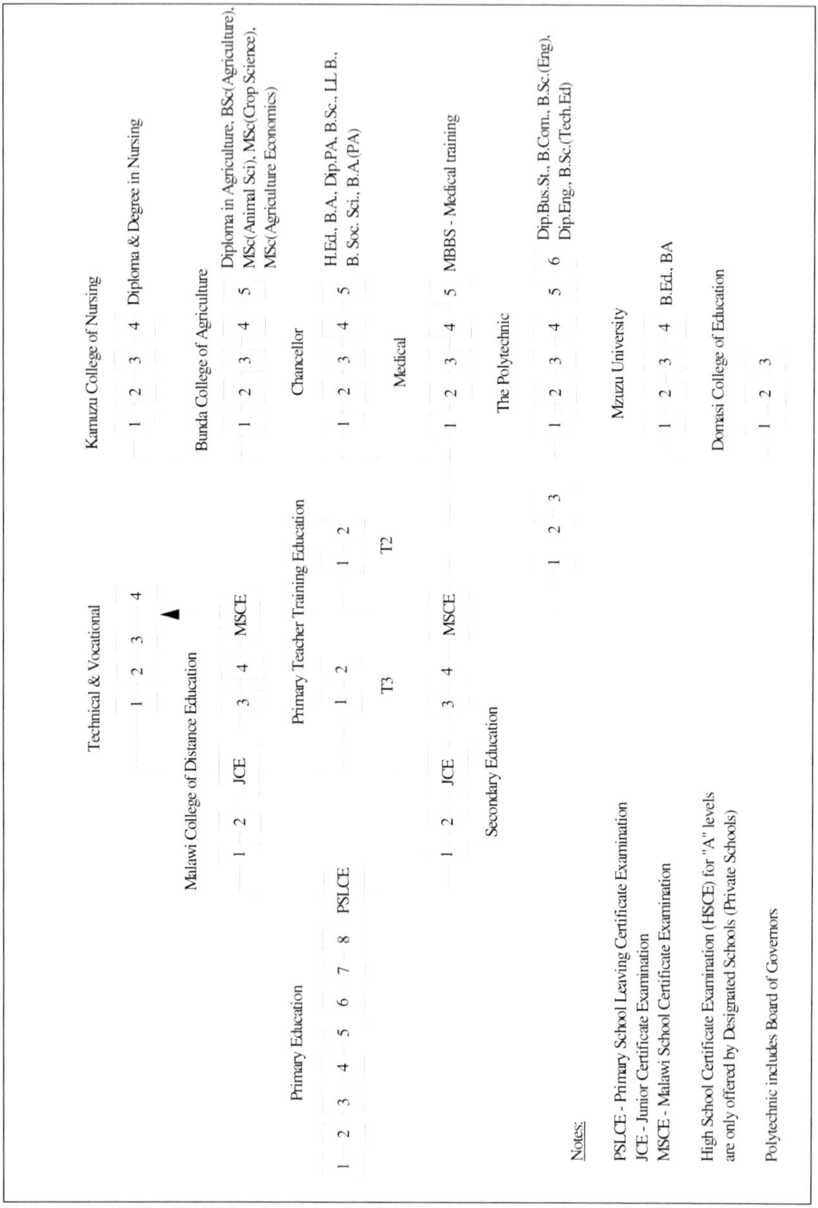

Source: MoE&VT 2006:3

App. 2: Interview Schedule for Community (ISC)

I, Anja Langer, would kindly like to ask for your assistance. I am a PhD-Student at the University of Leipzig, Germany and recently attached to the Faculty of Education at the University of Malawi, Chancellor College for research purposes.

The topic of my PhD dissertation is *"Mother tongue instruction as a means of promoting cognitive development of Primary school pupils in Malawi"*. Therefore, I would like to interview you on your perceptions about children's learning and cognitive development through the mother tongue.

In this attempt I am supported by the University of Malawi and GTZ. I thank you for your assistance and your will to answer the following questions from your own point of view and appreciate your honest responses!

Profession	
Date of Interview	

1. Sex Male Female
2. What is your highest level of education academically?

1	Never had formal education	☐
2	Primary School, Std 1-4	☐
3	Primary School, Std 5-8	☐
4	Secondary Forms 1-2	☐
5	Secondary Forms 3-4	☐
6	University	☐
7	Don't know	☐

3. Which languages do you speak and at what level?

Language	Mother Tongue	Fluent	Proficient	Working Knowledge
Chichewa	☐	☐	☐	☐
Ciyawo	☐	☐	☐	☐
Citumbuka	☐	☐	☐	☐
Other___________				

4. What is your understanding of "using the mother tongue of the children as medium of instruction"?
5. What language do you want your children to be taught in at school? Explain
6. What language is actually used? Which Standard?
7. Do you think the language (of learning and teaching) at school has any influence on the performance / results of your children? Explain
8. Which language do you use at home? Do you switch from one language to another? Which situations?
9. Do you think school prepares your children for the future? (for the society, for the daily life/problems)
10. Do you think school builds children's logical thinking?

App. 3: Interview Schedule Teachers (IST)

School / Position	
Date of Interview	

1. Sex Male Female
2. What is your highest level of education academically?

1	Never had formal education	☐
2	Primary Std 1-4	☐
3	Primary Std 5-8	☐
4	Secondary Forms 1-2	☐
5	Secondary Forms 3-4	☐
6	University	☐

3. Which languages do you speak and at what level?

Language	Mother Tongue	Fluent	Proficient	Working Knowledge
Chichewa	☐	☐	☐	☐
Ciyawo	☐	☐	☐	☐
Citumbuka	☐	☐	☐	☐
Other______________	☐	☐	☐	☐

4. What professional training do you have?
5. What is the first language or mother tongue of the majority of your pupils?
6. What is your understanding of "using the mother tongue of the children as medium of instruction"?
7. Have you recently been trained in the use of the mother tongue of the children for teaching? What was the nature of the training?
8. Do you think the current primary curriculum deliberately promotes the development of logical thinking in children? If yes, in what ways?
9. Which role does the language play?
10. What do you understand by "development of logical thinking in children" in the classroom?
11. In the setting of this work, logical thinking is defined as the child's ability to draw conclusions from rules s/he has learned, to work systematically as well as to generalize from the particular.
12. In what ways can logical thinking be facilitated or developed by the teacher in the (multilingual) classroom?
13. Do you think teaching in the mother tongue has any influence on the development of logical thinking? Explain.
14. In what ways did YOUR pupils show logical thinking in your lessons (LAC approach)?
15. What lesson activities do you think can enhance the development of logical thinking in pupils? Why?
16. What are some of the challenges in the development of logical thinking skills in the classroom?
17. Which activities did you often engage children in within the classroom? Why?
18. What language did pupils use among themselves when they are engaged in these activities?
19. Did you encourage your pupils to express their opinions? How? Which experiences did you make so far? What language did they use?
20. Did/do you feel any change in participation / motivation of the pupils when you switch(ed) from Chichewa to mother tongue during the lesson? Explain.

21. Control school: Did your pupils progress faster or without difference when the mother tongue was used as medium of instruction? Pilot school: Did your pupils progress faster or without difference when LAC was introduced compared to lessons before LAC?
22. How did you introduce new topics? Why?
23. Did you switch from one language to another? In which situations?
24. Did you give your pupils problems/tasks that they had not encountered previously? Why?
25. Did you encourage your pupils to ask questions? Explain (under what circumstances, etc)
26. How did you handle slow and fast learners in your class? (Giving faster learners more challenging tasks?)
27. In general, how does the school build children's logical thinking?

App. 4: Interview Schedule for Teacher Trainers (ISTT)

TTC / Position	
Date of Interview	

1. Sex Male Female
2. What is your highest level of education academically?

1	Primary Leaving Certificate	☐
2	JCE	☐
3	MSCE	☐
4	Degree	☐
5	Diploma	☐
6	Bachelor / Master	☐
7	PhD	☐
8	Other	☐

3. How long have you taught at your TTC?
4. Which languages do you speak and at what level?

Language	Mother Tongue	Fluent	Proficient	Working Knowledge
Chichewa	☐	☐	☐	☐
Ciyawo	☐	☐	☐	☐
Citumbuka	☐	☐	☐	☐
Other ___________	☐	☐	☐	☐

5. What is your understanding of "using the mother tongue of the children as medium of instruction"?
6. How do you touch the topic of cognitive development of pupils during your teaching? (Do you reflect on children's cognitive development while teaching your subject?)
7. Have you recently been trained in the use of child-centred methods? What was the nature of the training?
8. How does child-centred methods support the logical thinking of pupils?
9. Describe logical thinking in your own words. How can your pupils show their logical thinking in your classroom?
10. What kind of sources do you use for teaching? Are there publications on cognitive development in the Malawian context?
11. Do you think teaching in the mother tongue has any influence on the development of logical thinking? Explain.
12. Do you think the PCAR curriculum deliberately promotes the development of logical thinking in children? If yes, in what ways? What does it say about the language of instruction?
13. Do you encourage your pupils to express their opinions? How? Which experiences did you make so far? What language do they use?
14. Which activities can a teacher employ in order to develop children's logical thinking skills?
15. What strategies do you use to handle fast and slow learners in your class? (Giving faster learners more challenging tasks?)

16. Do you think there is any change in participation / motivation of the pupils in primary schools when the teacher switches from Chichewa to mother tongue during the lesson? Explain.
17. Do pupils progress faster or slower when the mother tongue is used as medium of instruction?

App. 5: Interview Schedule for Ministry Officials (ISM)

Position	
Date of Interview	

1. Sex Male Female
2. What is your highest level of education academically?

1	PSLCE	☐
2	JCE	☐
3	MSCE	☐
4	Degree	☐
5	Diploma	☐
6	Bachelor / Master	☐
7	PhD	☐
8	Other	☐

3. What is your specific task at the Ministry of Education?
4. What is your understanding of "using the mother tongue of the children as medium of instruction"?
5. What do you understand by "development of logical thinking in children" in the classroom?
6. Do you think teaching in the mother tongue has any influence on the development of logical thinking of the children? Explain.
7. Do you think teaching in the mother tongue has any influence on the learning of the children? Explain.
8. Describe logical thinking with your own words. How can pupils show their logical thinking in the classroom?
9. In what ways can logical thinking be facilitated or developed by the teacher in the classroom?
10. Have you heard about any change in participation / motivation of the pupils when teachers switch to the mother tongue?
11. Do you think school builds children's logical thinking?
12. Do you think the use of the mother tongue of the children for teaching is feasible in Malawian primary schools?

App. 6: Code ISC

0. Status
   1 Village Head
   2 Mother
   3 Father
1. Sex
   1 Female
   2 Male
2. Education
   1 No formal education
   2 Primary St. 1-4
   3 Primary St. 5-8
   4 Secondary Form 1,2
   5 Secondary Form 3,4
3. Languages spoken

	Chichewa	Ciyawo	Citumbuka	English	Citonga
Mother tongue	311	321	331	341	351
Fluent	312	322	332	342	352
Proficient	313	323	333	343	353
Working knowledge	314	324	334	344	354
Don't speak	315	325	335	345	355

4. MT as MoI
   1 Children acquire knowledge easier
   2 Children perform better (results)
   3 Better conversation between teacher and pupils
   4 Better understanding of concepts
5. MoI
   1 First MT, later other languages
   2 Chichewa (national language), English
   3"English is best" though problems in classroom
6. language used
   1 Mother tongue in lower classes
   2 Chichewa in most of the classes
   3 Mother tongue only sometimes because it is not authorized
   4 Mix mother tongue and Chichewa
   5 Chichewa and English
7. Language influence on performance
   1 Yes, children understand concepts and are proud of language
   2 Yes, when taught in mother tongue pupils can express themselves much better
   3 Yes, foreign language can disturb the learning
   4 Yes, language of textbooks is important as basis for teaching

8.1. Language at home
   1 Mother tongue

8.2. Switch to other language
   1 Arabic for religious studies
   2 Chichewa when visitors, reading books
   3 English with father of children
   4 No

9. Future preparation

1 Yes. Good education contributes to development of area

10. Logical thinking built

1 Those who go to school, are clever

2 Language and logical thinking are close connected

3 Mother tongue-pupils think better and faster

App. 7: Code IST

0. Position
   1 Teacher LAC
   2 Teacher Control
   3 Head teacher
   4 Teacher Demonstration school
1. Sex
   1 Female
   2 Male
2. Education level
   1 PSLCE
   2 JCE
   3 MSCE
   4 Bachelor / Master
3. Languages spoken

	Chichewa	Ciyawo	Citumbuka	English	Citonga
Mother tongue	311	321	331	341	351
Fluent	312	322	332	342	352
Proficient	313	323	333	343	353
Working knowledge	314	324	334	344	354
Don't speak	315	325	335	345	355

4. What professional training do you have?
   1 TTC
5. What is the first language or mother tongue of the majority of your pupils?
   1 Ciyawo
   2 Chichewa
   3 Citumbuka
6. What is your understanding of "using the mother tongue of the children as medium of instruction"?
   1 Able to understand concepts
   2 Pupils can express themselves
   3 Achieve the objectives of learning
   4 Easier learning, overcome frustration
7. Have you recently been trained in the use of the mother tongue of the children for teaching? What was the nature of the training?
   1 Yes. LAC project
   2 Yes, in TTC
   3 No
8. Do you think the current primary curriculum deliberately promotes the development of logical thinking in children? If yes, in what ways?
   1 Yes, involving learner-centred methods. Pupils are able to express their views.
   2 Yes, get and understand concepts, home experiences incorporated
   3 No, from other countries (UK) implemented
   4 Not quite, don't cater for use of language for easy understanding
   5 No, doesn't involve critical thinking
9. Which role does the language play?
   1 Big role. Children catch the concepts and context easier
   2 Pupils are able to express and understand and answer questions
   3 No break between home and school, easy cooperation among pupils
   4 No role.

10. Logical thinking is …
  1 ability to think
  2 knowledge before teacher teaches (from home)
  3 sharing ideas
  4 thinking straightforward to the point
  5 carry out activities from simple to complex
  6 critical thinking
  7 independent acting
  8 to follow instructions
11. In what ways can logical thinking be facilitated or developed by the teacher in the (multilingual) classroom?
  1 participatory methods
  2 discussions among pupils, role play
  3 responding to needs / abilities of pupils (identify slow/fast learners and assist them accordingly)
  4 through activities from simple to complex using real objects
12. Influence of MTE on the development of logical thinking
  1 Understanding between teacher and pupils, participation
  2 Ideas are grabbed quickly
  3 Activates creativity
13. In what ways did YOUR pupils show logical thinking in your lessons (LAC approach)?
  1 explain a problem to classmates (BOSS system)
  2 asking and answering questions
  3 bring resources into classroom, learn how to use them
  4 constructing sentences on their own with given words
  5 Arguing, discussing
14. Activities to enhance the development of logical thinking
  1 Matching pictures / words
  2 Drawings, Newspapers
  3 Puzzles, games
  4 giving new problems to look for solution
  5 group/pair work
15. What are some of the challenges in the development of logical thinking skills in the classroom?
  1 Shortage of materials
  2 "Ignorance of pupils" = not knowing, childishness
  3 different levels of pupils
  4 large classes, poor concentration
16. Activities you often engage children in within the classroom
  1 group works
  2 role play
  3 story telling and summarizing
  4 games, Maths text problems
  5 tasks solving on blackboard by pupils
17. What language did pupils use among themselves when they are engaged in these activities?
  1 mother tongue
  2 Chichewa, instead of MT. Encouraged to use Chichewa instead of MT (They can use MT at home) (IST III)
18. Express their opinions?
  1 Yes, but more in mother tongue
  2 Yes, but MT not welcomed (IST III)
  3 Yes, mostly after group discussions in MT.

19. Change in participation of the pupils when switch from Chichewa to mother tongue during the lesson?
   1 More participation, even shy pupils
   2 No. Pupils are discouraged to use MT (IST III)
   3 Difficulties to express some ideas in foreign language (English: short answers; MT: talking)
20. Pupils progress faster or without difference when the mother tongue was used as medium of instruction?
   1 Mother tongue > participation high
   2 No mother tongue because they will face problems later (IST III)
   3 Yes, faster in mother tongue
   4 Faster, but problems with end-of-year-examinations in English (St. 7)
21. How did you introduce new topics? Why?
   1 Songs, rhymes, drawings
   2 brainstorming, discuss in groups
   3 task given to discuss in group and come up with result
   4 Connecting with daily experience
22. Switch from one language to another
   1 No, when start in one language, end in same language
   2 Yes, to make points clear
23. Pupils are given problems/tasks that they had not encountered previously?
   1 Yes, to develop thinking capacity, challenge them
   2 Sometimes, to be active, to think
   3 Yes, to test their past experiences
   4 No
24. Encourage pupils to ask questions?
   1 Give them chance, ask
   2 shy pupils involved in activities
   3 After teaching time for feedback/reflection
25. How did you handle slow and fast learners in your class?
   1 Mix them in one group together
   2 Encourage slow learners to express themselves
   3 "Those who don't know anything, come in the afternoon" (IST III)
   4 different tasks and time to solve them
   5 Ask faster pupils to explain to slower pupils (BOSS-system)
   6 Fast learners an repeaters extra or rephrased tasks from textbooks
26. In general, how does the school build children's logical thinking?
   1 systematic work
   2 encourage smart work
   3 making experiences
   4 learn to decide, reason
   5 assessing achievement
   6 no answer

App. 8: Code ISTT

0. Position
   1 Lecturer
   2 Head of Department
1. Sex
   1 Female
   2 Male
2. What is your highest level of education academically?
   1 JCE
   2 MSCE
   3 Degree/Diploma
   4 Bachelor
   5 Master
3. How long have you taught at your TTC?
   1 1-4 yrs
   2 5-9 yrs
   3 10-14 yrs
   4 15-19 yrs
4. Languages spoken

	Chichewa	Ciyawo	Citumbuka	English	Citonga
Mother tongue	411	421	431	441	451
Fluent	412	422	432	442	452
Proficient	413	423	433	443	453
Working knowledge	414	424	434	444	454
Don't speak	415	425	435	445	455

5. What means "using the mother tongue of the children as medium of instruction"?
   1 Pupils learn easier in MT, grasp concepts
   2 Learners are free, but lack of sufficient terminology
   3 should be used up to higher level and nation-wide
   4 local languages in lower Standards, language can be a barrier
   to acquisition of knowledge, easy access and daily experience
6. How do you touch the topic of cognitive development of pupils during your teaching?
   1 Topic in EDF
   2 Testing according to Bloom's taxonomy
   3 Learning from concrete to abstract; modelling of ideas using real objects; practical approach (following Piaget)
7. Have you recently been trained in the use of child-centred methods? What was the nature of the training?
   1 InWEnt + MIE workshop on participatory methods
   2 InWEnt
   3 InWEnt + LAC
8. How do child-centred methods support the logical thinking of pupils?
   1 Direct link; pupils part of learning; develop formulas on their own
   2 Chance to explore things from known to unknown
   3 Learners contribute, are involved and develop skills

9.1. Logical thinking is …
   1 order your thoughts, each point brings you to the next
   2 rationale thinking, step by step
   3 thinking about consequences / results

9.2. How can your pupils show their logical thinking in your classroom?
1 Carrying out experiments step by step in groups
2 Drawing conclusions from rules they've learned
3 the way they answer, present; way they choose learning materials
4 discussions, arrange logical order after brainstorming

10. What kind of sources do you use for teaching?
1 Handbooks, Secondary school textbooks, experience
2 Books, meetings, colleagues

11. Do you think teaching in the mother tongue has any influence on the development of logical thinking? Explain.
1 Yes, learner-centred and MT, because pupils have to deal with new concept only, no language barrier
2 Yes, learner start from what they know to unknown
3 Yes, clear instructions help constructing concepts
4 Very difficult, not sure.

12. PCAR curriculum deliberately promotes the development of logical thinking in children?
1 No. TTC curriculum has changed but no materials (teacher guides, reference books) New teaching with old materials
2 Yes. Continuous assessment, learner work autonomous
3 Yes, challenging tasks make pupils think.

13. Do you encourage your pupils to express their opinions? How? Which experiences did you make so far? What language do they use?
1 Chichewa. In group work.
2 English. Encourage to criticise his teaching
3 English. Writing own assessment

14. Which activities can a teacher employ in order to develop children's logical thinking skills?
1 Making observations, conclusions, generalization in experiments
2 games, group work (discussing, arguing)
3 Exercises that use processes on different levels, creative with materials
4 practical activities to come up with formula

15. What strategies do you use to handle fast and slow learners in your class? (Giving faster learners more challenging tasks?)
1 Different levels of questions (thought provoking vs. simple)
2 In large classes slow learners have to suffer
3 Mixed groups, counselling
4 individual work and help for slow learners
5 extra exercises but pressure of work

16. Do you think there is any change in participation / motivation of the pupils in primary schools when the teacher switches from Chichewa to mother tongue during the lesson? Explain.
1 Yes, observable.
2 Yes, they are more free. Have ideas but keep quite because problem of proper vocabulary

17. Do pupils progress faster or slower when the mother tongue is used as medium of instruction?
1 Faster, get the concepts right, but tests are in Engl/Chichewa
2 Faster, observed through LAC

App. 9: Code ISM

0. Position
   1 Director Basic Education
   2 EMAS
   3 DEM
   4 PEA
1. Sex
   1 Female
   2 Male
2. Education level
   1 MSCE
   2 Bachelor
   3 Master
   4 PhD
3. Specific task
   1 monitoring / supervising
   2 curriculum implementation
   3 sensitisation of community
4. What is your understanding of "using the mother tongue of the children as medium of instruction"?
   1 communication in familiar language
   2 Mother tongue supports learning process
5. What do you understand by "development of logical thinking in children" in the classroom?
   1 ability to reason
   2 ability to follow activities systematically
   3 way children think and coordinate ideas
6. Do you think teaching in the mother tongue has any influence on the development of logical thinking of the children? Explain.
   1 pupils understand concepts / grasp objects of lesson
   2 increases ability to reason
   3 thinking is developed
   4 other languages confuse
7. Do you think teaching in the mother tongue has any influence on the learning of the children? Explain.
   1 supports understanding
   2 faster learning. No point of thinking about language and then expressing
   3 lesson objectives are understood
8. Logical thinking is …
   1 understanding and reasoning
   2 applying a concept according to age
   3 expressing oneself fully and following instructions
   4 solving problems
   5 imagining objects and modelling in Arts
9. In what ways can logical thinking be facilitated or developed by the teacher in the classroom?
   1 making use of a known situation (using realia)
   2 using participatory (learner-centred) methods
10. Have you heard about any change in participation / motivation of the pupils when teachers switch to the mother tongue?
    1 more active in mother tongue
    2 no
11. Do you think school builds children's logical thinking?
    1 yes. Giving challenging tasks

12. Do you think the use of the mother tongue of the children for teaching is feasible in Malawian primary schools?
   1 yes, but difficult *
   2 divides nation
   3 costly
   4 no

* Reasons:
   - not many fluent Ciyawo-speakers among teachers (ISM II)
   - might cause political tensions (ISM I)
   - Costly (ISM I)
   - Chichewa = National language; TTC training in Chichewa,
     English > difficulties to teach in mother tongue, too many languages in Malawi (ISM III)
   - some languages don't have (standardized) orthography (ISM IV)

App. 10: Tables for Test Evaluation

	Repetition rates in primary schools							
	Standard 1	Standard 2	Standard 3	Standard 4	Standard 5	Standard 6	Standard 7	Standard 8
Boys	26,09	21,99	22,85	17,81	16,78	13,24	11,27	16,31
Girls	25,40	21,17	22,35	16,88	16,13	13,44	11,71	14,48
Total	25,74	21,58	22,60	17,34	16,45	13,34	11,48	15,51

Table 2.1. Repetition rates in primary schools (Source: MoE&VT 2006:37)

	Dropouts in primary schools							
	Standard 1	Standard 2	Standard 3	Standard 4	Standard 5	Standard 6	Standard 7	Standard 8
Boys	21,67	5,71	15,28	12,53	15,27	13,51	10,44	8,61
Girls	22,42	7,00	14,53	11,84	15,96	14,95	18,78	22,76
Total	22,05	6,36	14,90	12,19	15,62	14,21	14,41	14,81

Table 2.2. Dropouts in primary schools (Source: MoE&VT 2006:39)

	Repetition rates in secondary schools			
	Form 1	Form 2	Form 3	Form 4
Boys	0,54	4,56	1,24	8,47
Girls	0,77	7,52	1,86	9,86
Total	0,65	5,97	1,49	9,03

Table 2.3. Repetition rates in secondary schools (Source: MoE&VT 2006:77)

	Dropouts in secondary schools			
	Form 1	Form 2	Form 3	Form 4
Boys	9,39	7,36	7,68	3,23
Girls	12,06	9,79	11,28	3,62
Total	10,61	4,02	9,11	3,39

Table 2.4. Dropouts in secondary schools (Source: MoE&VT 2006:77)

App. 11: Multilingual Education Models based on Bloch (2000: 32ff)

Standard	Mother tongue medium	English	Chichewa
1	Literacy, maths, content subjects	Subject	Subject
2	Literacy, maths, content subjects	Subject	Subject
3	Literacy, maths, content subjects	Subject	Subject
4	Literacy, maths, content subjects	Subject	Subject
5	Subject (optional)	Literacy, maths, content subjects	Subject

App model A1. Mother tongue as medium of instruction and English / Chichewa as subjects.

Standard	Mother tongue medium	English	Chichewa
1	Literacy, maths, content subjects	Subject	
2	Literacy, maths, content subjects	Subject	
3	Literacy, maths, content subjects	Subject	
4	Literacy, maths, content subjects	Subject	Subject (optional)
5	Subject (optional)	Literacy, maths, content subjects	Subject

App model A2. Mother tongue as medium of instruction plus two languages, but in phases.

Standard	Mother tongue medium	English	Chichewa
1	Literacy, maths, content subjects	Subject	
2	Literacy, maths, content subjects	Subject	
3	Literacy, maths, content subjects	Subject	
4	Literacy, maths, content subjects	Subject	Subject (optional)
5	Literacy, maths, content subjects	Subject	Subject
6	Literacy, maths, content subjects	Subject	Subject

App model A3. As model A2, but 6 years scenario.

Standard	Mother tongue medium	English	Chichewa
1	Literacy, maths, content subjects	Subject	Subject
2	Literacy, maths, content subjects	Subject	Subject
3	Literacy, maths, and 80% content subjects	Medium 20% content subjects for highly contextualised subjects e.g.: music, physical education, creative arts	Subject
4	Literacy, maths, and 70% content subjects	Medium 30% content subjects for highly contextualised subjects e.g.: music, physical education, creative arts	Subject
5	Subject and supportive medium	Literacy, maths, content subjects	Subject

App model B1. 5 years scenario with sporadic switch to English as medium of instruction from Standard 3.

Standard	Mother tongue medium	English	Chichewa
1	Literacy, maths, content subjects	Subject	
2	Literacy, maths, content subjects	Subject	
3	Literacy, maths, and 80% content subjects	Medium 20% content subjects for highly contextualised subjects e.g.: music, physical education, creative arts	
4	Literacy, maths, 70% content subjects	Medium 30% content subjects for highly contextualised subjects e.g.: music, physical education, creative arts	Subject
5	Literacy, maths, 30% content subjects	Medium 70% content subjects for highly contextualised subjects e.g.: music, physical education, creative arts	Subject
6	Subject and supportive medium	Literacy, maths, content subjects	Subject

App model B2. Mother tongue education, with gradual switch to English medium from Standard 3 to Standard 6 (or 7)

Standard	Ciyawo (class 1)	Content Subjects	Chichewa (class 2)	English as a subject	Subject additional local language
1	Literacy, maths	20% together bilingual, 80% MTI classes	Literacy, maths	Class 1&2 together	Class 1: Chichewa, Class 2: Ciyawo
2 and 3	Literacy, maths	30% together bilingual, 70% MTI classes	Literacy, maths	Class 1&2 together	Class 1: Chichewa, Class 2: Ciyawo
4	Literacy, maths	40% together bilingual, 60% MTI classes	Literacy, maths	Class 1&2 together	Class 1: Chichewa, Class 2: Ciyawo
5	Literacy, maths, 50% MTI, 50% English	50% together English, 50% MTI classes	Literacy, maths, 50% MTI, 50% English	Class 1&2 together	Class 1: Ciyawo, Class 2: Chichewa
6	Subject and supportive medium	100% together in English	Subject and supportive medium	Class 1&2 together	

App model C1. Mixed language situation in classroom; pupils are partly divided according to their mother tongue for instruction.

Standard	Ciyawo (group 1)	Content subjects	Chichewa (group 2)	English	Subject
1	Literacy, maths	Both languages, alternating	Literacy, maths	Subject	Group 1: Chichewa, Group 2: Ciyawo
2	Literacy, maths	Both languages, alternating	Literacy, maths	Subject	Group 1: Chichewa, Group 2: Ciyawo
3	Literacy, maths	Both languages, alternating	Literacy, maths	Subject	Group 1: Chichewa, Group 2:Ciyawo
4	Literacy, maths	Both languages, alternating	Literacy, maths	Subject	Group 1: Chichewa, Group 2: Ciyawo
5	50% Literacy, maths, 50% English	50% Both languages, alternating 50% English	50% Literacy, maths, 50% English	Subject	Group 1: Ciyawo, Group 2: Chichewa

App model C2. Mixed language situation with a teacher who has a good command in both languages and switches between the languages.

App. 12: Multilingual Education Models based on MoEST (2003a:44ff.)

Standard	Chichewa	Another Malawian language	English
1	Medium of instruction	Subject	Subject
2	Medium of instruction	Subject	Subject
3	Medium of instruction	Subject	Subject
4	Medium of instruction	Subject	Subject
5	Subject	Subject	Medium of instruction

App model Chichewa-dominated school environment

Standard	Ciyawo	Chichewa	English
1	Medium of instruction	Subject	Subject
2	Medium of instruction	Subject	Subject
3	Subject	Medium of instruction	Subject
4	Subject	Medium of instruction	Subject
5	Subject	Subject	Medium of instruction

App model Non-Chichewa-dominated school environment

App. 13: Pictures from the data collection (Langer 2010:163ff.)

Primary school pupils who participated in the tests in Chiole

The Team: Catherine Mwanachawa, Anja Langer, Maxwell Mawelu, Linda Bwanali

Pupil carrying out the subtest *Isolating objects, positive*

Pupil carrying out the subtest *Pictoral stories*

Pupil carrying out the subtest *Continuing sequences*

Pupil transferring the rule during the subtest *Analogy sequences*

Images

Tables

Abbreviations

ADEA	Association for the Development of Education in Africa
BEP	Basic Education Project
BIVA	Bildbasierter Intelligenztest für das Vorschulalter – Picture-based Intelligence test for preschool level
CERT	Centre for Educational Research and Training
CLS	Centre for Language Studies
DEM	District Education Manager
DTED	Department of Teacher Education and Development
FPE	Free Primary Education
GTZ	Deutsche Gesellschaft für technische Zusammenarbeit – German Technical Cooperation
IPTE	Initial Primary Teacher Education
JCE	Junior Certificate Examination
LAC	Literacy Across the Curriculum
MBTL	Malawi Breakthrough to Literacy
MIE	Malawi Institute of Education
MIITEP	Malawi Integrated Inservice Teacher Education Programme
MoE (MoESC)	Ministry of Education, Sports and Culture
MoEST	Ministry of Education, Sports and Technology
MoE&VT	Ministry of Education and Vocational Training
MRE	Ministry Responsible for Education
MSCE	Malawi Secondary School Certificate Examination
NRO	Nongovernmental Organisation
PCAR	Primary Curriculum and Assessment Reform
pers.	personal talk

PSLCE	Primary School Leaving Certificate Examination
SACMEQ	Southern African Consortium on Methods for Quality Education
TTC	Teacher Training College
UNESCO	United Nations Educational, Scientific and Cultural Organization
UNICEF	United Nations Children's Education Fund